P

MW01596105

'This is unquestionably **the** source of information for any bride and groom-to-be... covering absolutely everything that can make a wedding special. The One Stop Wedding Kit is so well organized that, despite the myriad of topics it covers, anxious brides will easily find whatever they need right at their fingertips.'
The New York Times

'I recommend this book to all our brides. Jam packed with great ideas, insider tips, checklists and advice, it steers you clear of disaster and makes organising your wedding so simple a child could do it.'
Lynne Scanlan, Senior Wedding Coordinator for Couran Cove Resort Australia, winner of over 20 national and international awards

'Dazzle your friends with a fairytale wedding – without going bankrupt. The One Stop Wedding Kit saves you from stress, dramas, wasted time and money down the drain. Read this book before you plan another thing.'
Michelle Crane, Revisions Editor for London's top publishing houses

'The One Stop Wedding Kit saved me thousands of dollars and made planning my dream wedding fun and easy. It's a Godsend for busy brides!'
Trish Stephenson, Events Coordinator for Australia's most awarded wedding venues

Also by Jessica Howe

One Stop Wedding Readings – Published May 2006

Jessica is the founder of Love and Cherish, a company dedicated to helping busy brides turn their dream day into reality. For your wedding tip of the day, red hot promotions and practical advice on stress-free, easy wedding planning visit her website at www.loveandcherish.net.

The One Stop Wedding Kit

by Jessica Howe

Cover artwork by Matt Wells
Illustrations by Liberty Browne

Published by Love and Cherish

ISBN 0 9775524 0 3

Love and Cherish
32/336 Boundary St
Spring Hill
Q 4000
Australia

publish@loveandcherish.net
www.loveandcherish.net

For my beautiful husband Rob, who made me the happiest
bride in the world the day we were married.

Our gift to you...

As a valued customer we would like to offer you a copy of
The Bride's Essentials, worth $13, absolutely free. With this
fabulous gift you can:

- Prevent wedding day stress with our fully customisable
  wedding day timeline
- Delegate tasks with printable copies of every checklist in
  this book
- Celebrate in style with our comprehensive Engagement
  Party Checklist

To download this fabulous gift just go to www.loveandcherish.
net/gift and enter your date of purchase and the promotional
code **print_ed_013**.

Where the one man loves the one woman
And the one woman loves the one man,
The very angels desert heaven and sit in that hour
And sing for joy

Braham-Sutra

Contents

Introduction

As a bride-to-be you're about to embark on one of life's most amazing journeys – one that will take you on a rollercoaster of emotions. This book is designed to make the ride of your life as fun, easy and stress-free as possible.

The One Stop Wedding Kit comes in two parts – the Bride's Countdown at the front and the main chapters which explore each aspect of wedding planning. The **Bride's Countdown** on page 17 reveals exactly what to do when so you won't forget a single detail. Each 'to do' cross references a page that tells you how to plan that element of your day. The **main chapters** are packed with inspiration, ideas, advice and cost saving tips, as well as **checklists** to use when talking with suppliers, and even a **glossary** to help you out with 'wedding speak' you aren't familiar with.

Armed with this book you can rest assured that your wedding day will be everything you desire. So get comfortable, top up your champagne glass and let's get started!

Wishing you love, laughter and a lifetime of marital bliss,

Bride's Countdown

Bride and Groom: As soon as possible	Page	Done?
Set wedding budget.	51	
Agree on the approximate number of ceremony and reception guests.	43	
Decide on ideal wedding date and time.	36	
Announce your engagement.	31	
Plan your engagement party. For a free engagement party checklist, go to www.loveandcherish. net/gift and enter promotional code print_ed_ 013.	45	
Choose your engagement ring.	32	
Agree on the style and theme of your wedding.	59	
Decide between a religious and civil ceremony.	149	
Draft guest list for ceremony, reception and evening (include reserves).	43	
Choose your ceremony venue.	152	
Choose an officiant and arrange to book the service with them.	151	
Start a health and beauty regimen and a diet and exercise plan.	243	

Bride and Groom: As soon as possible	Page	Done?
Purchase wedding insurance.	-	
Choose and book the reception venue.	173	
Arrange marquee hire if necessary.	-	
Choose bridesmaids and page boys.	39	
Choose and book photographer.	207	
Choose and book videographer.	218	
Choose witnesses.	-	
Choose best man and groomsmen.	39	
Edit these countdown checklists as needed and circulate them to all involved, briefing them on duties, timings and venues. For printable copies of these lists, a customisable wedding day timeline and lots more, go to www.loveandcherish.net/gift and enter promotional code print_ed_013.	-	
Get ideas for your wedding flowers and choose a bouquet style.	133	
Other:		

Mother of the Bride: As soon as possible	Page	Done?
Send an announcement of your daughter's engagement to your local newspaper and arrange for an article to appear.	32	
Together with the bride and her father, decide on the number of guests to be invited to the ceremony and reception.	43	

Mother of the Bride: As soon as possible	Page	Done?
Inform the groom's mother of the numbers of guests and ask for her to forward a list of people she would like invited.	-	
Together with the bride and groom, finalise the guest list.	43	
Help the bride choose flower arrangements for the ceremony and reception.	133	
Assist the bride as necessary.	39	
Other:		

Bride and Groom: 6 months or more before the wedding	Page	Done?
Advise attendants of their duties.	41	
Bride: Find and buy your wedding gown.	69	
Book DJ, band or other entertainment.	199	
Bride: Arrange attire for female attendants.	84	
Arrange attire for groom and male attendants.	82	
Bride: If using a dressmaker, book them now and choose fabric and patterns.	69	
Groom: Book transportation for wedding day and going away.	125	
Choose and book your florist.	145	
Make catering arrangements.	184	
Other:		

19

Bride and Groom: 6 months or more before the wedding	Page	Done?

Bride and Groom: 3-6 months before the wedding	Page	Done?
Decide on wedding invitations and stationery.	91	
Bride: Buy wedding gown, accessories, bridesmaid dresses and outfits if not being made.	69	
Buy wedding rings and arrange insurance cover for them.	36	
Decide on honeymoon – where and how long?	265	
Start discussing what sort of wedding cake you want and go to cake tastings.	188	
Write your wedding vows if you've decided not to follow the traditional wording.	165	
Discuss ceremony and order of service with officiant.	169	
Discuss music options for the ceremony.	158	
Select menu and wine, and advise caterers and reception venue of guest numbers and food and drink requirements.	184	
Book musicians and singers for the ceremony.	158	
Book reception staff if required.	-	
Decide whether to have a wedding website and start putting it together.	101	
Start selecting items for gift list.	227, 231	

Bride and Groom: 3-6 months before the wedding	Page	Done?
Order your wedding cake.	188	
Hire or purchase clothes for the groom and male wedding party.	82, 86	
If marrying in church, ask your minister for the dates for publishing the banns in the bride and the groom's church.	-	
Notify appropriate register office of intended marriage.	-	
Finalise and register your wedding gift list.	227	
Inform the mother of the bride and bridesmaids where your gift list is registered so they can field enquiries.	99	
Record each wedding gift as it arrives and who sent it in this book's Gift Recorder so you know who to send thank you letters to.	236	
Order printed order of service booklets.	91, 114	
Confirm passports are up to date.	266	
Obtain travel visas if required.	-	
Book time off work for honeymoon.	266	
Organise pre-honeymoon inoculations and medication if required.	266	
If inviting guests from abroad, send out their invitations now.	100	
Other:		

Mother of the Bride: 3-6 months before the wedding	Page	Done?
Order the bride and groom's preferred wedding stationery.	97	
Continually update the groom's family on how the arrangements are progressing.	-	
Together with the bridal couple and father of the bride, organise the reception, including food, drink and entertainment.	176	
Assist the bride as necessary.	-	
Other:		

Father of the Bride: 3-6 months before the wedding	Page	Done?
Together with the mother of the bride and bridal couple, organise the reception, including food, drink and entertainment.	176	
Assist the bride as necessary.	-	
Other:		

Bride and Groom: 1-3 months before the wedding	Page	Done?
Book accommodation for your wedding night.	-	
Bride: Buy wedding gift for your groom, brides-maids and pageboys.	-	
Groom: Buy wedding gift for your bride, best man and groomsmen.	-	
Decide on reception decorations and order them including balloons, disposable cameras and favours.	177	
Order confetti, rose petals, doves or butterflies if releasing them.	156	
Check honeymoon arrangements and tickets.	265	
Prepare a map to include in your invitations and on your wedding website (if you have one)	99, 101	
Arrange hospitality and transport for out of town guests.	-	
Bride: Together with the mother of the bride, write, address and send out invitations together with any maps, directions, details of local hotels and details of wedding website (if you have one).	47	
Record acceptances and refusals.	-	
Make arrangements for pets with neighbours or kennels.	-	
Agree with attendants where they will dress on your wedding day.	-	
Send an announcement of your wedding to the local newspaper and arrange for a report of your wedding to appear.	-	
Bride: Arrange final fitting of wedding dress, bridesmaids' dresses and pageboys' outfits.	-	

Bride and Groom: 1-3 months before the wedding	Page	Done?
Choose and buy your shoes and accessories.	76, 79, 81	
Book a practice session and appointment with your hairdresser and makeup artist.	250, 255	
If applying your own wedding day makeup, buy cosmetics and start practising now.	252, 255	
If self catering, make detailed shopping, cooking and freezing plans.	-	
Acknowledge replies to invitations as they come.	-	
Agree/confirm wedding rehearsal with all involved.	-	
Arrange accommodation, tourist and wedding information for out of town guests.	-	
Ask the best man and chief bridesmaid to arrange hen & stag nights, and inform those invited of the dates.	46	
Choose your entrance music for the reception and give it to the venue staff.	183	
Choose your 'must-have' music from your DJ or band's song list	199	
Feeling overwhelmed? Relax with our chill-out tips.	258	
Other:		

Chief Bridesmaid: 1-3 months before the wedding	Page	Done?
Organise the bridal shower.	46	
Organise the hen night.	46	

Mother of the Bride: 1-3 months before the wedding	Page	Done?
Send out wedding invitations to all guests including the groom's parents, enclosing directions, details on transport, accommodation and wedding website URL (if having one). Note that whilst enclosing details of the bridal registry with the invitations is not technically proper etiquette, it is becoming increasingly common and accepted for modern brides to do this.	99	
Assist the bride in keeping an up to date list of who is attending and who has declined.	-	
On request, give out details of the bridal registry.	99	
Use the Gift Recorder supplied and record all gifts in it as they arrive.	236	
Help any guests requiring special attention in arranging their transport or accommodation, such as lift sharing.	-	
Send out invitations to the reserve guest list as you receive 'unable to attend's.	-	
Other:		

Groom, father of the bride and best man: 1-3 months before the wedding	Page	Done?
Prepare speech for reception.	-	
Assist the bride as required.	-	
Other:		

Bride and Groom: 2-4 weeks before wedding	Page	Done?
Call those guests you haven't heard from to check if they will be attending.	-	
Check the bride's father and best man have prepared their speeches.	-	
Advise the florist of the final number of button-holes and corsages.	140	
Inform the reception venue and caterers of the final number of guests.	-	
If you plan to use your car for the wedding/honeymoon, check it's in good working order.	-	
Wear in your wedding shoes and scuff the soles with sandpaper to avoid slipping.	81	
Final fittings for attendants.	-	
Prepare a wedding day timeline and distribute to all members of the bridal party. You can download and print out a customisable wedding day timeline from www.loveandcherish.net/gift (please enter promotional code print_ed_013).	-	
Choose and practise your first dance	201	
Prepare ceremony cards for the first two front rows.	168	
Other:		

Bride and Groom: 2-4 weeks before wedding	Page	Done?
Other:		

Mother of the Bride: 2-4 weeks before	Page	Done?
Take custody of presents that arrive early.	202	
Assist the bride as required.	-	
Other:		

Bride and Groom: 1-2 weeks before	Page	Done?
Ensure all attendants know their duties.	39	
Final check on all honeymoon plans.	266	
Collect banns certificate from your officiant.	-	
If having a church wedding, deliver order of service booklets to church for the officiant, choir and organist.	-	
If you haven't done so already, send marriage announcement to local newspaper and post it on your website.	-	
Enjoy your hen night.	-	
Final check on all clothing.	69	
Groom enjoys his stag night.	-	
Check reception details, confirm final numbers and special dietary requirements.	173	

Bride and Groom: 1-2 weeks before	Page	Done?
Wrap gifts for attendants, parents and groom.	-	
Attend practice session with hairdresser and makeup artist (preferably on the same day)	250, 255	
Final check on arrangements for flowers, transport, venue & entertainment.	133, 125, 176, 197	
Hold a wedding rehearsal with attendants.	169	
Arrange for hired items to be returned after wedding.	-	
Create the final seating plan.	193, 117	
Advise chief groomsman of seating plan.		
Advise attendants what time they should arrive at your home on your wedding morning so there's plenty of spare time to get ready and relax.	-	
Find out the storage requirements for your cake, and arrange for it to be transported to your reception venue on the day	192	
Other		

Bride and Groom: Day before the wedding	Page	Done?
Delegate last-minute tasks.	-	
Check the going away car will be in the right place at the right time.	-	
Pack for honeymoon.	268	
Give gifts to the best man and attendants.	-	
If self catering, do any last-minute defrosting and shopping.	-	
Pack going away clothes and leave the suitcases in a convenient place so they can be taken to reception.	-	
Lay out your wedding dress, accessories and jewellery.	-	
Arrange for your cake to be delivered to the venue and assembled.	192	
Organise a safe place for gifts brought to the reception to be stored.	-	
Enjoy the wedding rehearsal dinner.	47	
Eat healthy food, drink lots of water, relax and have an early night.	-	
Other:		

Getting Started

Not long from now you'll be blissfully gliding down the aisle looking stunning beside your new husband. It's enough to make anyone feel overwhelmed, so how do you get yourself on track?

This chapter will guide you through the first steps of planning your big day. It gives tips on how to select the best date and time for your wedding, reveals how to announce your engagement and shows you the stress free way to compile your guest list. Discover how to select a quality engagement and wedding ring – and most importantly, how to assemble a team of helpers who will keep you sane and help you at every turn, right up to your big day.

Spreading the Good News

Now you're engaged you're probably dying to tell everyone – but just hold your horses! Traditionally the bride's parents are the first to be told, followed by the groom's. Many couples nowadays prefer to invite both sets of parents to dinner and tell them together.

Next you'll want to tell your siblings, and then you can draw up a list of all the friends, family and colleagues you'd like to announce your engagement to. Most brides prefer to tell their friends face to face or over the phone so they can hear their reaction. Email or text messaging is not recommended as it's too impersonal.

Newspaper announcements

You may want to ask your parents to place a formal announcement in your local paper. If your groom's parents live in a different city, his parents can announce it in their local paper too.

Local and national newspapers have different protocols for how engagement announcements are worded. The announcement will also be phrased differently according to your family situation (for example if your parents are divorced or if one parent is deceased). Your newspaper will tell you the correct wording for your own situation when you contact them to place the announcement.

Choosing your Rings

The practice of giving engagement rings goes far back to the days when they were made of grass and later leather, stone and rudimentary metals. It was the early Egyptians who began placing the ring on the forth finger as they believed a vein in this finger led straight to the heart.

The engagement and wedding ring are undoubtedly a bride's most cherished pieces of jewellery. They are the only part of your wedding ensemble that you will wear for the rest of your life, so they deserve to be selected carefully. For this reason most couples choose to shop together to ensure they both get exactly what they want.

Gold

Gold is the traditional favourite and is measured in carats. The higher the carat the purer the gold, but the purer the gold the softer it is, causing it to scratch more easily. If you want a ring you can wear every day, choose a hardwearing one of no more than 18 carats.

Platinum

Platinum is a heavy, very hard wearing white metal which unlike gold is used in an almost pure form and will not tarnish over time. If you or your fiancé have metal allergies, platinum is the clear choice as it's hypoallergenic. It is however significantly more expensive than gold.

One Stop Tip

Consider how your ring will look as you age – cutting edge fashion could be tomorrow's embarrassment.

Diamonds

Diamonds are of course the classic choice of stone for engagement rings. When choosing your ring's design, consider your own sense of style. If you tend to dress quite glamorously a big rock could suit you, but if you're a jeans and T-shirt kind of girl perhaps you'd prefer something more discreet.

There are also practical considerations. A high-set diamond catches the light beautifully, but is inclined to get caught on clothing and is more likely to come loose of its setting. If you choose this style you may need to remove your ring when performing household chores.

When it comes to diamonds, bigger is not always better. The key to selecting a quality rock is to consider the four Cs:

Cut   The cut of a diamond gives it its multi-faceted sparkle, so a well cut diamond reflects light and twinkles with brilliance. There are several different cuts to choose from, the most popular being the classic Round or Brilliant cut.

Colour   Diamonds are graded on a colour scale, which ranges from D to Z. The more colourless the diamond the greater its value. Rare colourless diamonds are rated D, whilst E, F, G, H, I and J are near-colourless. After that the colour becomes more noticeable and the diamond is less valuable.

Clarity   Diamonds have flaws, or 'inclusions' as they are known, which can disrupt the flow of light through them. As you would expect, the fewer the flaws the better. You can recognise a diamond with no major flaws as it appears bright and unclouded to the naked eye.

Carat   This is the diamond's weight. Alone it does not dictate the value because a less heavy diamond with better clarity, colour and cut will be worth more.

Your gemstone's setting

It's vital that you choose a setting which holds your gemstones securely, so when making your selection remember the following:

- Six claws are safer than four
- A bezel (rub-over) setting is safer than a claw setting
- A heavier setting is stronger than a light setting
- A lower setting is less likely to be damaged than a higher setting

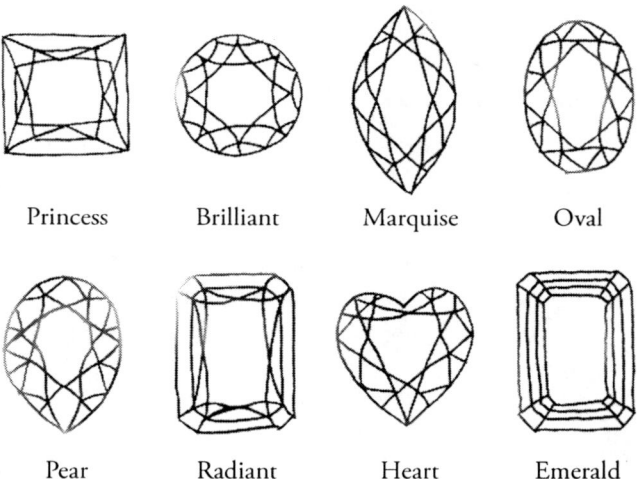

Princess   Brilliant   Marquise   Oval

Pear   Radiant   Heart   Emerald

Other gemstones

Although diamonds are the most popular stone for engagement rings, they are by no means your only choice. There are plenty of other beautiful gemstones such as the sapphire, a highly durable stone and one which was given to the Queen Mother, Queen Elizabeth and Princess Anne on their engagements. Sapphires exist in almost every colour, from cornflower blue to yellow, orange and pink.

However the stone which has been associated with love and marriage longer than any other is in fact the pearl. A lustrous pearl looks stunning set in an engagement ring and it flatters almost every skin tone. And if you want something truly personal, why not have your engagement ring set with your birth stone?

One Stop Tip

An engagement ring usually looks best if made from the same metal as the wedding ring.

Questions for your Jeweller

☐ What are their return, warranty, insurance, cleaning and repair policies?

☐ Is the price negotiable? (it often is)

☐ Is there any cost for resizing, and if so how much?

☐ Can you make your purchase conditional on getting an appraisal of the ring from a third party to confirm its value?

One Stop Tip

Ask your jeweller for a written appraisal of your ring so you can give it to your insurance company.

Setting the Date

Once you're engaged one of the first things you will want to do is to set a date. A good place to start is by choosing a general time of year.

Has a particular month or season always seemed particularly romantic or picturesque to you? It might be spring when the blossom trees are in bloom, autumn when the leaves have just started to fall, or winter when the cool air makes everything feel fresh and crisp. Think of weddings you've been to which you really enjoyed. Did the season or time of day make it seem extra special, and if so how?

Day of the week

Most couples marry on a Saturday so their guests can attend without having to take time off work. Friday is also a good option as your guests can drink and party without having to worry about work the next day. Marrying on a weekday can be a good way to save money, since many wedding professionals will give discounts if asked – and the less keen guests will not attend! Just check your key guests are available on that day.

Date

There might be a date which has special significance to you both, like the anniversary of your first date or the day you met. However steer well clear of:

- Dates with sad associations for you or your family
- Tourist season or school holidays
- Your honeymoon location's monsoon season
- Religious restrictions determined by your faith (Catholics, for example, are discouraged from marrying on Sundays and holy days)

Lead time

Check there is enough time to plan the sort of wedding you want. If there is not, many of the best ceremony and reception locations will be fully booked. Twelve months or more should be sufficient, but you can plan your wedding in less time if you are flexible with your choice of venues.

Time of day

According to an old Chinese tradition it is best to marry on the half hour, as the rising hand of the clock will bring you luck. Perhaps more importantly in the modern world, rush hour is best avoided.

An early morning ceremony may mean guests have to travel up the night before, and you and your bridal party will be up at the crack of dawn to get ready. It also means organising hours and hours of entertainment for your guests if the party is to last into the evening without fizzling out.

On the other hand timing the ceremony too late in the day may mean it all goes past in such a blur that you hardly get the chance to enjoy it! The best time for your ceremony is therefore probably somewhere between 12pm and 4pm.

One Stop Tip

If you have your heart set on a particular venue, consider confirming availability and booking it before you announce the date of your wedding.

Wedding Date Checklist

- ☐ Will the weather be appropriate at your chosen time of year?
- ☐ Is your ideal ceremony and reception venue available on that day?
- ☐ Is your officiant free?
- ☐ Have you left yourself enough time to plan the sort of wedding you want?
- ☐ If you have a favourite wedding flower, is it in season?
- ☐ Are all the key people able to attend – parents, brides-maids, best man, best friends and family?

- ☐ If there are guests coming from abroad, is this date possible for them?
- ☐ Will the date coincide with your period?
- ☐ Can you both get the time off work for your honeymoon?

Assembling your Team

Even if you want to make many of the wedding arrangements yourself, it will help enormously to have the support of trusted friends and family. This is the one time in your life when everyone will be falling over themselves to help, and feel proud and honoured when asked. So right from the start, put a trusted team together whose help you can rely on.

The Mother of the Bride

Most brides plan their weddings in conjunction with their mothers, who usually welcome the prospect of helping out with plans and feel honoured to be involved. Chances are your Mum will be delighted by the prospect of all those shopping trips, dress fittings and lunches with her daughter. However some couples prefer to pay for and organise their wedding without parental involvement so they can avoid family squabbles and do not have to compromise on the kind of day they have.

The Mother of the Bride is usually involved at every stage of planning the wedding so the division of responsibilities is very much up to you. Traditionally however her main responsibilities are to:

- Inform everyone involved of their duties
- Choose her own outfit
- Arrange the printing of the invitations and send them
- Order the wedding cake

- Book the reception venue
- Hire the photographer and videographer
- Find a florist
- Arrange the evening entertainment
- Arrange accommodation for out of town guests

The groom

It might come as a surprise that your groom wants to be heavily involved in the planning. Granted, he might not care whether you choose lilies or roses, but he'll certainly have an opinion on the honeymoon location!

If he's the technical type he might want to create a wedding website and select a photographer and videographer. If he enjoys the finer things in life perhaps he wants to pick the wine list, choose the menu and accompany you to cake tastings. And even if he has no clue about planning, he may jump at the chance of organising the honeymoon or finding a DJ.

Traditionally the groom's duties are to:

- Choose the engagement and wedding rings with the bride
- Assist the bride wherever possible
- Choose the best man and groomsmen
- Hire the morning suits
- Order flowers for the bride, bridesmaids and mothers
- Arrange cars to and from the ceremony
- Give notes to the head groomsman on where to seat close relatives at the ceremony
- Make honeymoon plans and all necessary travel arrangements (reservations, tickets, accommodation, visas and passports etc.)
- Give the church fees to the best man to pay after the ceremony

- Prepare his speech including the bridesmaids' toast
- Buy gifts for the best man, groomsmen and child attendants
- Buy a present for the bride

The Chief Bridesmaid

Your chief bridesmaid, or maid of honour as she is often known, will no doubt be a real source of support and advice throughout the coming months. Apart from helping out generally her traditional responsibilities are to:

- Run errands and help with any shopping that needs to be done
- Organise and attend the pre-wedding parties
- Help the bride to dress for the ceremony
- Assist the other attendants and flower girls
- Precede the bride to the ceremony to arrange the bridesmaids
- Hold the groom's ring and the bride's bouquet during the ceremony
- Arrange the bride's veil
- Assist the bride during the reception, checking her hair and make-up
- Help the bride to dress into her going-away clothes
- Help send out wedding cake to friends not present
- Assist the mothers of the bride and groom throughout the day
- Help out with child attendants and make sure they are safe

The bridesmaids

Don't forget your other bridesmaids, who are no doubt

waiting in the wings to be asked for help. Ask them to help organise pre-wedding parties, advise on flower choices and accompany you on shopping trips and to dress fittings. They will probably be so excited they'll want to be involved in as much as possible. Traditionally however their duties are to:

- Help the bride and her family during wedding preparations and particularly on the wedding day
- Assist with any child attendants
- Mingle with the guests at the reception

The Father of the Bride

Your proud father also has his part to play. Traditionally he is responsible for:

- Writing his speech
- Accompanying the bride to the church in the last car
- Giving the bride away
- Ensuring the comfort of all guests
- Socialising with the groom's family and other guests at the reception

The Best Man

Apart from generally assisting the groom, the best man's duties are to:

- Double check transport arrangements
  Organise the delivery and return of the men's wedding suits
- Organise and attend the stag party at least one week before the wedding, ensuring the groom is looked after responsibly
- Get the groom to the ceremony in plenty of time

- Stand next to the groom during the ceremony and hand him the rings at the appropriate moment
- Be an official witness at the signing of the register
- Pay the church fees with money given to him by the groom
- Ensure all guests have transport to the reception
- Make sure guests arriving to the reception are given drinks
- Assist the photographer by organising guests for the group shots
- Make his speech and read out any messages
- Make sure the bride and groom leave the reception in good time for their onward trip
- Keep all tickets and passports safe for the honeymoon and hand them to the groom at the appropriate time
- Help pack the "going-away" car with the couple's luggage

The Groomsmen

The groomsmen, or 'ushers', will be of most assistance on the day of the wedding when they should help out as needed. Apart from this their traditional duties are to:

- Assist the groom and best man before and during the wedding
- Escort guests to their seats at the ceremony
- Mingle with the guests at the reception
- Escort or direct guests to their tables at the reception

Drawing up the Guest List

If either set of parents are contributing to the wedding costs, it's only fair to involve them in choosing who will be invited. See it from their point of view – they are probably so proud their child is getting married that of course they want their closest friends to share in their joy.

Here is a step by step way of drawing up your guest list which should keep everyone happy.

Step 1 – Involve the parents

Decide on your ideal number of guests. Then draft your own list of who you would like to invite and ask your parents and your groom's parents to do the same.

Step 2 – Cull the list

Once you have all three lists, get together and start pruning. Openly discuss the relationship you have with each person now and what future you see for it. Never feel obligated to invite someone you have known for years but are no longer close to, or to return the favour just because they invited you to their wedding.

Step 3 – Compromise

If the situation gets heated, compromise by suggesting a quota of guests for each set of parents to invite. For example you might want to allow each side of the family to invite a quarter of the guests, with you and your fiancé choosing the remaining half.

Step 4 – Estimate numbers

Remember that not everyone who is invited will be able to come, particularly if they are elderly or live abroad. To get a good idea of how many guests will actually attend, go through your list and tick those who you are sure will be there. Count them up and you will have a rough idea of how many people will attend on the day. If you want more guests than that, simply add more people to your list.

Step 5 – Don't forget…

As a matter of courtesy you should invite the officiant and his or her spouse, so make sure you include them in your calculations. And don't forget to add yourselves to the list so you have accurate numbers!

One Stop Tip

If you and your fiancé are hosting the wedding yourselves, drawing up the guest list is easy. Just invite who you want – and score some extra brownie points by asking both sets of parents if there's anyone special they want you to invite.

Pre-Wedding Parties

The run-up to your wedding day will be full of excuses to celebrate. Whilst some events are organised by friends, others like the engagement party are hosted by the couple themselves or their parents. It's up to you how many parties you have. Here's an outline of each event so you can take your pick.

The engagement party

This usually takes the form of a fairly informal gathering at the bride's or bride's parents' house, or at a local restaurant. Traditionally it is hosted by the bride's parents, but where this is not possible the groom's parents may act as hosts. Many modern couples – particularly those who live together – choose to host their own engagement party. For a sample wording of an engagement party invitation, see the Stationery chapter.

One Stop Tip

Some couples forego an engagement party and save the big party until the wedding day, preferring instead to celebrate privately with a romantic long weekend away.

The bridal shower

This is a chance for the bride's closest friends and family to gather together and 'shower' the couple with gifts for their new household. The bridal shower is usually hosted and organised by your chief bridesmaid, and it takes place around a month before your wedding.

Usually only the bride's close friends and family are invited to the shower. Traditionally it is an all-female event, although the groom often attends. You may however like to break with tradition and join the growing number of brides who opt for a couples shower.

If you are sending out formal invitations see the Stationery chapter for advice on how they can be worded.

The hen and stag parties

The hen and stag parties are typically organised by your chief bridesmaid and the best man. They are paid for by each guest who attends, so you may want to let them know how much money will be involved and who this should be given to. Formal invitations are not usually sent.

The rehearsal dinner

The wedding rehearsal is often held the day before the wedding and offers an opportunity to run through your big day's sequence of events. The groom's parents usually host the rehearsal dinner afterwards. Only the bridal party and sometimes out of town guests are invited. If you want to send invitations they should complement but not compete with your wedding invitations. Again, the Stationery chapter will advise you on the wording.

One Stop Review

- ☐ Announce your engagement first to your parents, next to your siblings and then your friends and family.
- ☐ Place an engagement announcement in your local paper.
- ☐ Select quality rings which match your everyday look and lifestyle.
- ☐ Pick an appropriate date for your wedding day.
- ☐ Choose your bridal party and assemble a support team who are keen to help at every turn.
- ☐ Draft your guest list with input from both sets of parents.
- ☐ Stay on track with what needs to be done when by using the Bride's Countdown at the start of this book.
- ☐ Use the checklists in this book when you meet wedding professionals. For printable copies go to www.loveandcherish.net/gift, enter your date of purchase and the promotional code print_ed_013.
- ☐ Delegate tasks by printing out and distributing checklists from your Bride's Countdown (again, printable copies are available on the Love and Cherish website).

Notes

Notes

Affording It

After the proposal comes the harsh realisation: turning your day into reality will take cold, hard cash. Talk about unromantic! But rest assured – there are ways to have your dream wedding without breaking the bank. It will just take a little more time, patience, creativity and bargain hunting. This chapter will reveal how to make budgeting for your wedding a simple, painless process.

Where do I Start?

Your first step is to see how much money you and your fiancé can dedicate to wedding costs from your monthly salaries. Multiply this by the number of months left until your wedding day, and add on any savings you can contribute.

Speak to the parents

Now you know how much you can save, arrange a meeting with your parents and a second one with your groom's parents. Tactfully ask them how much money they can contribute, and gracefully accept whatever they offer. Add your own contribution to that of your parents' and you have your wedding budget.

Start prioritising

Now you just need to break this down into each element that needs to be paid for. Every couple has different priorities for their wedding day. Some want a big party with a live band and free flowing champagne; others prefer to spend their money on a spectacular honeymoon. Once you have calculated your budget you can decide where to splash out and where to save.

Keep It Real

List every element of your day that needs to be paid for. Crank up the budget on those which are important, and reduce it for those which aren't. Play around with the list until the bottom line corresponds to your overall budget. When you've finished, take your budget with you when you go shopping.

Save automatically

Make saving easy by setting up a standing order with your bank. This is also sometimes known as a bank deposit or direct transfer. It should automatically transfer your monthly wedding contribution into a high-interest account. Arrange for the transfer to take place directly after your salary is paid so you are not tempted to spend it.

Plan for unexpected costs

However carefully you plan there will always be hidden costs such as postage fees for stationery and payments for dress alterations. Build in a buffer from the outset, and accommodate spending around 10% more than you expect.

> ### *WHO PAYS FOR WHAT?*
>
> Traditionally the bride's parents would shoulder the majority of the wedding costs, but nowadays the reality can be quite different. Often both sets of parents and the bride and groom contribute. If you and your fiancé have lived together for some time you may even prefer to pay for the whole wedding yourselves.

Tight Budgets

If the amount you have to spend falls short of the average cost of a wedding there are still lots of options open to you. With careful planning you can still have a beautiful wedding. Try some of the following to make your funds stretch further.

Reduce the guest list

You can cut your costs considerably by keeping your guest list down to just the people who really matter to you. What's more, inviting fewer people means you can lavish more food and wine on each guest.

Increase your lead time

There's nothing wrong with setting a date two years from now. If you give yourself more time to save up you can have your dream day without cutting corners. You'll also have more time to plan it.

Decrease the cost per head

The highest proportion of any wedding budget goes on food and drink. If you want to cut costs, think carefully about how much you can afford to spend on each person. Choosing cheaper meal and wine alternatives makes a big difference to the overall cost.

Limit your reception guests

Invite everyone to the ceremony, but only close friends and family to the reception. That way you can enjoy a large wedding ceremony with all your friends but limit the cost of food and drink.

Build rapport

The best piece of advice for brides on a tight budget is to treat the wedding professionals you deal with kindly and build a rapport with them. If you love their work then tell them so, and openly apologise for your small budget. You will be amazed at the discounts you are offered by taking a friendly, genuine approach rather than the neurotic diva-like attitude these people are used to from some brides!

Our guarantee

We believe every bride deserves the very best on her wedding day, whatever her budget. To help your funds stretch further you'll find lists of 'Cost Saving Tips' throughout this book. We guarantee these techniques will enable you to hold a beautiful, lavish wedding for a fraction of the usual cost – without compromising on style. What more could a bride ask for?

One Stop Review

- ☐ Work out how much you have to spend.
- ☐ Decide where to splash out and where to save.
- ☐ Build in a buffer for unexpected costs.

- [ ] Save automatically with a standing order.
- [ ] Use the 'Cost Saving Tips' in each chapter.

Notes

_____

_____

_____

_____

_____

_____

_____

_____

_____

_____

_____

_____

_____

_____

_____

_____

_____

_____

_____

_____

_____

_____

_____

_____

_____

_____

_____

Notes

Developing a Theme

Choosing a theme for your wedding day is one of the first and most important things you need to do. Your future decisions on venue, dress and decoration will all be guided by it.

Your wedding is a unique statement about who you are as a couple so this chapter will show you how to pick a theme which is uniquely yours, reflecting your own style, desires and beliefs. You will learn how to weave details and unique touches throughout, to make your day a completely individual celebration of your personality and passions in life.

Where do I Start?

First take a moment to think about what kind of wedding you want. What aspects of your personalities do you want your day to reflect? If you are both laid back and casual, perhaps a very formal event would not suit you. A cheerful, happy couple may envision their wedding day as a joyful, fun celebration whereas a more romantic pair might prefer an intimate candle-lit gathering.

Express your beliefs

Your wedding day should express the beliefs closest to your

heart. Perhaps you both value a close-knit family, have a passionate concern for the environment or share similar spiritual or religious beliefs. These fundamental values bind you together as a couple, so think carefully how you can express them in your day.

Feature your interests

Fascinated by old-style movie glamour? Then pick a wedding dress fit for the silver screen and commission your photographer to take Hollywood style black and white shots. If you both share a fondness for a certain historical period or musical genre, you have the beginnings of a theme. And if you are both academic types who met at university, why not get married there?

Decide on the feel

Do you envisage something formal and respectful or joyful and fun? An environment of opulence and splendour, or homeliness and comfort? A relaxed ambience or one charged with vibrant energy? List the feelings which sum up your perfect day and brainstorm how you can express them.

WHAT'S YOUR WEDDING STYLE?

☐ Traditional	☐ Informal	☐ Exotic
☐ Modern	☐ Formal	☐ Intimate
☐ Colourful	☐ Flamboyant	☐ Pretty
☐ Opulent	☐ Relaxed	☐ Original
☐ Chic	☐ Fun	☐ Glamorous

Suggested Themes

Now you have decided on the elements of your day, it's

time to choose a theme. This should reflect a style and mood in keeping your personal tastes. Choose something close to your heart and stick to one theme rather than confusing everyone with several. Here are some ideas to get you started.

Romance

Unashamedly pretty and feminine, the appeal of the romantic vintage look lies in its nostalgia, sensuality and timeless beauty. A rose garden or a grand manor house are ideal locations.

You could decorate stationery with pressed flowers or the flowing motifs of early 1900s Art Nouveau. Fill every part of the day with pretty touches – floral prints, feathers, satin, chiffon, antique jewellery, delicate beaded bags and sparkling diamanté. Adorn tables with shimmering organza overlays sprinkled with fresh rose petals. Combine with gently glowing frosted candle holders or nightlights wrapped in Chantilly lace. To complete the look, add glass bowls overflowing with full-blown peonies in soft pastel shades.

Simple and elegant

Many brides dream of a chic, stylish celebration which epitomises sophistication, grace and elegance. Achieve this look by keeping colours to a minimum and focusing on shape, form and texture. Clean lines, simple flower arrangements, a sleek, modern wedding dress and elegant location are all key elements.

White on white is a classic take on this look. Add dimension with an accent colour like silver. Try combining white plates, white napkins wrapped with silver ribbon, silver candlesticks and silver cutlery on a white tablecloth.

Choose simple, sculptural centrepieces like tulips or lilies, or float flowers in water to highlight the sparkling silver and glassware. Thoughtful use of lighting can create a sophisticated, intimate dining experience. Keep table decorations simple and striking and wrap your bomboniere in thick, embossed white paper or feathery tissue.

The Great Outdoors

More and more couples are marrying outdoors in gardens, on the beach, in a forest or on a golf course. Choosing a place you both love to spend time can be a great way to individualise your day.

Nature lovers could tie the knot under ancient oak trees or in a rainforest. Send out invitations printed on handmade, petal encrusted paper, scatter pebbles on the tables and tie bomboniere with large fresh leaves and natural grasses.

If you have always loved the sea you could marry on a beach, by a lighthouse or at the end of a pier. Send 'message in a bottle' invitations, dress the bridal party in jade, turquoise and dusky blues and transfer guests to a stylish waterfront venue reception by cruise boat, yacht or even in a local fishing boat.

One Stop Tip

Marrying outdoors has long been popular in the US and Australia but the UK still prohibits it. If you live in the UK and want to marry outdoors consider tying the knot in a gazebo, or why not marry overseas?

Colour

Theming your wedding around a colour is an excellent way to coordinate all the elements of your day and make it look great in those all-important photos. Perhaps you have a favourite flower you would like to base your colour scheme around? Alternatively you can team contrasting colours like turquoise bridesmaid dresses with bright yellow bouquets.

Feature your theme colour in bright overlays on the reception tables or accessorise classic white linen with colourful bomboniere, flowers and place cards. Use vibrant colours like fuscia, red or blue to transform your reception venue into a riot of colour.

Choosing a colour that is in fashion will make it much easier for you to find bridesmaid dresses, favours and invitations to achieve your desired look. Make sure the colour you pick is one that suits your complexion, as you will be surrounded by it in the photos.

Cultural Heritage

Why not take your cultural heritage as your starting point? This works particularly well if you and your groom have different ethnic backgrounds as you can build in a little of both. The day then becomes a celebration of your union as two individuals whilst also symbolising the marriage of two cultures.

Feature dances, songs or wedding rituals from your country of origin. Serve up Granny's favourite recipes and hire roaming musicians to play traditional folk music. Including traditions with a special meaning to you is sure to make your wedding uniquely memorable as well as being a fascinating cultural experience for your guests.

Grand Affairs

For those who yearn for the glamour of yesteryear there's nothing like holding your wedding in a grand ballroom or stately home. There are many magnificent buildings to choose from, often with stunning outlooks.

You could consider marrying in a traditional winery overlooking the vineyard, at your city's art gallery or other heritage building. Many heritage hotels have spectacular chandeliers, ornate mirrors or spiral staircases in the lobby which make great backdrops for your photographs.

Invitations could be embossed, embellished with gold leaf detail or stamped with a wax seal. String strands of pearls through silver candelabras at the centre of each table. Serve lavish food like caviar and seafood and book a Swing band to perform.

Seasons

You may like to take the time of year as your inspiration. **Springtime** is the season for fresh colours, breezy fabrics and pretty pale posies. Hold your reception in a marquee with the lingering scent of just-cut grass, and decorate tables with pale blue gingham tablecloths and fresh flower buds. Alternatively dress tables in white, and accent with pale green and lavender flowers, bomboniere and place cards.

A fun **Summer** theme could be expressed with bright yellow sunflowers, yellow bridesmaid dresses and a yellow open-top sports car to whisk the happy couple away at the end of the night. For a more tropical feel decorate with bold colours, bright exotic blooms and glowing paper lanterns. You could even string the bridal table with vibrant garlands of tropical flowers.

Conjure the feel of **Autumn** with deep jewel tones of ruby, gold and chocolate. Integrate pine cones, cinnamon sticks, chestnuts, apples or pears into flower arrangements. Use pressed leaves for place cards.

For a White **Christmas** theme, choose somewhere with a

roaring open fireplace and decorate with holly wreathes and flickering candlelight. Hang mistletoe in doorways and dress tables with silver cutlery, red roses, ivy and twinkling fairy lights. Position ice sculptures around the room and serve a traditional Christmas roast followed by mince pies and Christmas pudding.

Be bold, be personal and be stylish. Whatever your theme, make it something you find beautiful that reflects the uniqueness of your personalities, your shared interests and passions in life.

One Stop Review

☐ Think about the core beliefs and values which bind you together.

☐ Consider your common interests.

☐ List the feelings which sum up your perfect day and brainstorm how you can express them.

☐ Choose a style that reflects your personality.

☐ Decide on a theme which can successfully incorporate all these elements.

Notes

Notes

What to Wear

Every bride wants her wedding gown to represent the epitome of wedding style. It needs to be beautiful and distinctive, yet comfortable and affordable. This chapter will reveal how to buy a stunning designer gown for a fraction of the list price. You will discover how to choose a neckline which flatters your figure, a colour which compliments your skin tone and jewellery that highlights your best features.

But dressing a wedding doesn't stop there – you have your groom and bridal party to think of too. Find out how to coordinate your whole bridal party, from the bridesmaids to the parents, so everyone looks simply stunning on your big day.

The Dress

The white wedding gown is a surprisingly modern tradition. Most nineteenth century brides would simply wear their best dress to church, often woven in bold colours. Over time however the white dress became a symbol of purity which presented the bride as a protected and valuable treasure.

Finding your dream dress can seem a daunting task – there are so many expectations riding on your choice! And when you do pluck up the courage to venture into a bridal salon, the huge selection of gowns can feel quite overwhelming. However with patience and advice from trusted friends, the search for your bridal gown can be a moving and memorable experience.

Where do I start?

What kind of gown you wear will set the look for the rest of your bridal party, so start with yourself before you think about anyone else. List the shapes, necklines and colours which usually suit you. Use these as your starting point, but don't disregard other styles just yet. A gown you would never have considered may look fabulous once you try it on.

Consider your wedding style

The venue, time of year and formality of the occasion will all influence your choice of dress. On the other hand don't be confined by convention. If you are marrying outdoors but still want to wear a full, floor length gown the contrast could look dramatic and original.

Visit some bridal shops

Make appointments with two or three bridal salons during their quiet times. Go armed with an open mind and a trusted friend or family member, and be prepared to make several of these outings. Indulge yourselves by discussing the day's findings over lunch or coffee.

Ask for advice

Engage shop assistants, many of whom have years of experience dressing brides. Ask them to pick the one dress from the whole shop that would suit you best, regardless of what you have asked for. After dressing hundreds of brides they usually have a good idea of what will suit your shape, and you may be pleasantly surprised by that slinky dress you would never normally have looked at. To give you an idea, here's a summary of which styles suit which figures.

Tall and slender	Try a fitted bodice and a full skirt which falls from a natural waist. A sheath, a-line or mermaid style will also suit you. If you like your neck and shoulders show them off in a strapless gown or one with delicate spaghetti straps. Whatever you choose, wear your height with pride – pull your shoulders back and hold your head high as you walk down the aisle.
Petite	An empire line will give you a slim silhouette and make you look taller. A sheath dress, a-line or halter neck will also give you the illusion of height. Elongate a short waist with a mermaid silhouette, and if you want to wear sleeves make sure they are long and not too tight. A very full skirt should be avoided.
Pear shaped	A ball gown or a-line style will look good. Strapless, portrait and off the shoulder necklines work well as they accentuate your upper body, whilst a basque bodice will slim the waist and hide full hips. Avoid anything that clings to the hips and tummy like a mermaid or sheath gown.

Full bust	To minimise a large bust draw attention downwards with a slightly dropped waist and a full skirt, and reserve any detail for the lower part of the dress. If you want to show off your bust, try a sweetheart or scoop neckline. Steer well clear of spaghetti straps, empire lines, strapless styles and ball gowns.
Small bust	Create the illusion of cleavage with twisted or gathered fabric, or subtly enhance your bust line with a square neckline. If you have good posture and shapely shoulders, try a strapless style. An empire line gown or bateau will also be flattering. Sweetheart necklines should be avoided, as should spaghetti straps if you have bony collarbones.
Broad shoulders	You can narrow this area with thick straps or a v-neck. Alternatively, show off your back and play down your shoulders with a halter neck. Avoid off the shoulder styles and spaghetti straps as these will make your shoulders look wider.

BRIDAL GOWN DEFINITIONS

A **Ballgown** has a fitted bodice and a very full, princess-style skirt. The **A-line** on the other hand is fitted through the bodice with a skirt which is slightly flared. A **Mermaid** gown is fitted throughout until it flares out just below the knee, whereas a **Sheath** dress has a narrow, figure hugging silhouette right the way to the floor. The **Empire line** is a high-waisted style which flares out from just below the bust.

Spaghetti straps   Halter neck   Off the shoulder   Scoop

Necklines

Spaghetti Straps

Thin, delicate shoulder straps which just support the bodice.

Halter neck

Backless with a single strap which wraps around the neck, or a high-necked style with deep armholes.

Off the shoulder

The sleeves fall just below the shoulders.

Scoop

A low, rounded neckline with a U shape.

Strapless   Square   Bateau   Sweetheart   Portrait

Strapless

A bodice without straps which finishes just above the bust.

Square

A half-square shaped neckline.

Bateau

A high neckline which curves downward slightly below the collar bone.

Sweetheart

Dips to a heart shape at the bust line.

Portrait

A wider version of the scoop neck, falling at the tip of the shoulders.

WEDDING DAY LINGERIE

It's important to get the right bust support and enhancement or the right dress can look wrong. Choose your lingerie after your gown so you know what kind of support you need - this is a great time to get a professional bra fitting. Treat yourself to something pretty or sexy, and for a perfect fit wear your wedding day lingerie to dress fittings.

Choosing a colour

Wedding gowns come in an incredible array of colours, and the right shade can transform even a very simple dress into something that really lights up a bride. If there's a hue that makes your skin look radiant or highlights your eyes, why not wear it for your wedding? Silver, crimson, lavender, gold and pastel shades put an original spin on the classic white dress.

If like most brides you have your heart set on a more conventional shade there are even more options open to you. The failsafe way to find the perfect match is to try lots of colours until you find one that makes your skin glow and your eyes shine. See the boxed text for some ideas.

WHICH HUE FOR YOU?

Dark skin suits stark white or blue white, which is the brightest shade of white with a very faint blue undertone. Also try diamond white or any very pale colour. **Tanned or golden skin** looks good in cream and bluish white. Blush, a warm peachy-pink hue, is an unusual alternative which makes **olive skin** glow beautifully. Those with **Pinkish complexions** should try diamond or natural white but avoid cream. **Blue-eyed blondes** will suit bluish white as it brings out the colour of their eyes, whilst **redheads** look radiant in ivory or gold.

One Stop Tip

Hang your gown on a pretty silk coat hanger on the day of your wedding. Your photographer may want to photograph it before you wear it, and it will look much more attractive than it would on a wire coat hanger.

Cost Saving Tips for your Dress

- For a beautiful gown at a fraction of the usual cost, call upmarket bridal salons and ask for the dates of their next sample sale. At these times they heavily discount their current range to sell it off quickly and make room for new collections.
- If you want something simple, buy a cream coloured evening dress from an upmarket store. Many are half the cost of a bridal gown – and just as elegant.
- Some of the more exclusive bridal salons send their gowns to discount outlets. Call round and ask where they get sent to.
- Shop at bridesmaid dress shops and buy a simple gown which you can dress up with embroidery or glamorous accessories.
- A figure-hugging dress will always cost less than a full-skirted one as it requires less material.

Headpieces

Your wedding day may well be the one opportunity you have in your life to wear a veil or tiara. Use the shape and style of your dress as inspiration and check your headpiece matches any jewellery you want to wear.

Veil

The veil was originally worn by women in the East to ward off the Evil Eye. Returning crusaders brought it back to Europe where it came to signify a bride's purity and innocence. In traditional marriage ceremonies the bride would remain veiled until the vows had been said, when the veil was lifted for the couple's first kiss, celebrating their first moment as husband and wife.

These days wearing a veil gives the bride an aura of mystery and a romantic, ethereal appearance. Veils are generally made of lace or tulle and the more formal the dress, the longer the veil. Try on several lengths at a bridal salon to see which one best suits you and your dress.

Flyaway

Many layered, barely reaching to the shoulder.

Blusher

Single layered, falling to the shoulders.

Elbow

Extends to the elbows.

Finger Tip

Grazes the fingertips.

Ballet

Drops below the bride's knees but above her ankles.

Chapel

Reaches all the way to the floor.

Cathedral

The longest of veils, falling to the floor with a slight train.

Tiara

Tiaras bring a regal elegance to any wedding ensemble. From simple crystal ornamented combs to full blow crowns, there is bound to be one just right for you.

You could choose to coordinate your tiara with the beading on your dress or the crystals in your earrings or necklace. Try lots of styles until you find one that best complements your dress.

> ## One Stop Tip
> If you want to wear real diamonds but can't afford them, check in the Yellow Pages for places where you can hire the real thing.

Other Headpieces

If you aren't a tiara kind of girl there are many beautiful alternatives. Fresh or artificial flowers woven into your hair look stunning in an outdoor setting. Hair jewels or dainty clips can bring sparkle to an up-do, or thread strings of pearls through your hair for a classic vintage look.

Jewellery

Pearls, crystals, diamonds, semi-precious stones – there's a dazzling array of exquisite jewellery out there for the modern bride. And whilst some will take this opportunity to invest in a striking necklace which can be worn again, there is plenty of charming jewellery out there for brides on a budget.

Less is More

Your accessories should be chosen to compliment your dress. A very simple gown can look dazzling teamed with a dramatic vintage necklace or eye catching chandelier earrings. The golden rule here is the more elaborate your gown, the simpler your jewellery.

Match the style

Use your dress as your starting point and choose jewellery which highlights its detail. You might choose a crystal-encrusted tiara which matches crystals on your bodice, or a pearl necklace which sets off the pearl detail around your neckline.

Accentuate your best features

Jewellery can be used to draw attention to your best features. Why not use stylish earrings to show off pretty ears? Or if you have a long neck and shapely shoulders, team a choker necklace with a stylish strapless gown.

If you can't make it, fake it

If you want to wear diamonds but can't afford them, think about buying some quality costume jewellery. The trick is to find something which looks like the real thing and might just about be affordable. A simple rhinestone pendant or drop earrings are ideal. Anything with hundreds of rhinestones will look unconvincing.

Keep your eyes peeled

Bridal salons are the obvious places to look for accessories but the great thing about wedding jewellery is you can find it almost anywhere. Raid Granny's jewellery box, rummage through antique shops and keep an eye out for unusual trinkets in boutique costume jewellery stores. If you still can't find what you want, consider having something specially made for the occasion.

One Stop Tip

You can remember family members who have passed away by wearing something of theirs on your wedding day, so you can feel they are with you in spirit.

Cost Saving Tips for your Accessories

- Borrow a veil or tiara from a recently married friend – just check the colour matches that of your dress.
- Ask your mother or grandmother if they have any jewellery that might be suitable. Wearing a string of pearls or brooch that has been in the family for some time not only saves you money but adds a chic, personal touch to your ensemble.
- Search out unusual jewellery or hair accessories from vintage shops.
- Buy quality costume jewellery which looks like the real thing.

Shoes

Gone are the days when bridal shops were the only place to find wedding shoes. Nowadays high street shoe shops are a great place to start your search. They often carry more fashionable lines than bridal boutiques, and at substantially lower prices.

Some shops have an area specially set aside for bridal footwear in glamorous satins and silks, often decorated with twinkling rhinestones, ribbon and fine embroidery. There may even be a handbag to match.

For fabulous footwear that looks and feels great, just follow these simple guidelines:

☐ Bring a swatch of your dress fabric when shopping for shoes so you can match the exact colour.

☐ Choose something comfortable which won't make you tower over your groom. Your heels should be high enough to look elegant but low enough to be comfortable if worn all day.

☐ Choose your footwear with your location in mind. For example thin, high heels will sink into grass or sand.

☐ To avoid slipping on the dance floor, scuff the soles of your new shoes with sandpaper or an emery board.

☐ Take your shoes with you to your dress fittings so the hem of your dress can be altered to the right length.

☐ Most importantly, wear your shoes in around the house so you are comfortable on your wedding day.

One Stop Tip

Pack some plasters in your wedding handbag which can be used in the event of blisters, and a spare pair of tights or stockings in case of ladders.

Groom and Groomsmen

There are plenty of options for the stylish modern groom. Just keep the theme and colour scheme of your wedding in mind and consider what level of formality will be appropriate.

Buying a tailored suit

If your groom wants to wear a lounge suit he should consider buying one. Off the shelf suits can be reasonably priced but a specially tailored suit will set you back upwards of US$800, so this is not a cheap option. It will however get many years of wear, each occasion bringing back happy memories of your wedding day.

Hiring a suit

On the other hand hiring a suit may only cost in the region of US $100 including tie, shirt and waistcoat. Hiring also makes it easier to match the style of a formal wedding. After all buying a morning suit is a waste of money since your groom will only rarely get the chance to wear it.

Matching the groomsmen

Hiring also means your groom can, if he wishes, be dressed the same as his groomsmen. It is not compulsory for the groom to match his groomsmen – in fact he'll stand out more if he wears something different. Preferably however the groomsmen's suits should match each other. If you are happy with them wearing their own dark suits they should at least wear matching ties and buttonholes.

Update your look

There's plenty of variety for modern grooms who want something a little different. Try mixing things up with a champagne, crimson or midnight blue shirt in silk or linen. There's a dazzling selection of waistcoats in an array of colours and rich textured fabrics such as satin or velvet brocades. Your groom's tie can be chosen to match either the bridesmaids' dresses or the bride's gown.

Choose a style

Professional hire companies will advise on style, fit and alterations to help take the guess work out of the exercise. Looking through a large formalwear shop's catalogue or website will give you an idea of what each style looks like and which occasions they are appropriate for.

Suit the occasion

The style of suit your groom selects will depend on the

formality of your wedding. Although you may want to keep your wedding gown a secret from him until the big day, he will at least need to know how formal it is as this will guide him in what he chooses to wear. Here are some general guidelines, but don't be afraid to break with tradition.

Formal daytime ceremony	Bride wears floor length gown with train and veil	Groom wears morning suit
Formal evening ceremony	Bride wears floor length gown with train and veil	Groom wears white tie and tails or a dinner suit
Semi-formal daytime ceremony	Bride wears floor length or ankle length gown with hair accessories or veil	Groom wears dinner jacket or lounge suit with dress shirt and tie
Casual wedding	Bride wears suit or cocktail dress with hat, short veil or hair accessories	Groom wears suit and dress shirt

Bridesmaids

Many brides choose to reflect their theme colour in their bridesmaids' dresses. Coordinated with bouquets and corsages, this works brilliantly in photographs.

Hit the shops

Your bridesmaids will know which styles suit their figures so ask for their help. Shopping for dresses with them can be great fun in the run-up to the wedding. It also allows them to bond with each other if they're not already close friends.

Choose a style

Your bridesmaids' dresses should compliment, but not necessarily mirror your bridal gown in shape and style. They should certainly not be more formally or elaborately dressed than you.

If they have different body shapes, buy different styles in the same colour so everyone gets to look good. If they have different skin tones, choose varying hues of the same colour. For example pale blue looks great with light complexions whilst dark blue suits darker skin tones.

Dress for the occasion

Broadly speaking, floor length bridesmaids' dresses are appropriate for a formal wedding and cocktail dresses are appropriate for a semi-formal one. If you are having a casual wedding you can either opt to dress your bridesmaids in cocktail dresses or, if you are wearing a suit, suits which compliment yours.

Find coordinating shoes

When it comes to shoes, use the colour of your bridesmaids' dresses as a starting point. Some shades like cream will be easy to match, and if you're having difficulty there are places that will dye a plain white pair of shoes any colour your heart desires.

Put a fabric swatch from your bridesmaids' dresses in your purse and keep your eyes peeled. If the colour you've chosen is in fashion you may find what you're looking for in a high street shoe shop.

Ask them to wear their own

If your bridesmaids will be wearing floor-length gowns in a colour which coordinates with black shoes, you could encourage them to wear their own as most women own a pair of dressy black heels. The fact that they aren't wearing the same style will probably go unnoticed under a long dress.

Choose other accessories

Discuss jewellery with your bridesmaids – they may already own something appropriate. For purses, hair accessories and wraps, raid shops like Accessorize to find something in a matching colour. You could also speak to your florist about wiring some flowers for their hair to match their bouquets.

Parents

Parents are often overlooked in the excitement of dressing bridesmaids and groomsmen. However if you have a strong colour theme, it may be important to you that their clothes coordinate with everything else. Including a little of your theme colour in their outfits can also make your parents feel much more a part of your day.

Mothers

Mothers usually want to buy a new outfit for their son or daughter's wedding, and dressing them in hues which compliment your bridesmaids can look stunning. If you handle it the right way you can make them feel special, pampered and involved. They will probably relish the opportunity of all those shopping trips with you to hunt down the perfect little outfit. Once again, remember it will be easier to find something suitable if your theme colour is in fashion.

There's no reason for both mothers to wear the exact same shade as your bridesmaids. Instead they might choose clothes in deeper or paler shades of that colour so it compliments their complexions and fits their own sense of style.

MOTHERS WHO KNOW BETTER

Some women have very firm ideas about what they will wear, so talk to both Mums soon after you announce your engagement. Tell them which colours you are thinking of using, and see if they would be willing to wear something in that colour. If they're not in to the idea, forget it. After all you don't want to start a family feud by insisting on what your mother-in-law wears to your wedding.

Fathers

For the dads, it might simply be a case of asking them to wear their own dark suits with a tie and buttonhole which matches your wedding colour. Make sure you arrange for their buttonholes to be delivered to them on the day. Appoint someone to help attach them, as sometimes nerves make this a little tricky.

One Stop Review

- ☐ Choose a bridal gown which embodies your theme, flatters your figure and compliments your skin tone.
- ☐ Next find a headpiece, jewellery and shoes which complete your look.
- ☐ Encourage your groom to ask a formal hire shop for advice on styles and levels of formality.

☐ Get some input from your bridesmaids on what styles best suit them.

☐ Don't forget the parents – they want to look good too!

Notes

_____

_____

_____

_____

_____

_____

_____

_____

_____

_____

_____

_____

_____

_____

_____

_____

_____

_____

_____

_____

_____

_____

_____

_____

_____

_____

_____

_____

_____

_____

_____

Notes

Wedding Stationery

The envelope feels heavy as you excitedly break the seal. Silver lettering catches the light, glinting like something precious as you run your fingers over crisply embossed script. Even the traditional wording has a time honoured significance which sends a shiver of anticipation down your spine.

Receiving a wedding invitation has always been a special and privileged experience. Originally wedding stationery was hand crafted by Medieval European monks, experts in the art of calligraphy, who were hired for this special task by esteemed royal and noble families. At a time when most people were illiterate, elaborately made invitations demonstrated a family's wealth and status.

Today, just as then, the invitation sets the tone for the wedding. All other stationery takes its cue from it. For best effect your invitations should reflect the feel, level of formality and colour scheme of the day.

Every bride wants to announce her wedding in style, and this chapter will show you how to do just that. It will help you navigate the confusing subject of invitation etiquette, guiding you step by step through the process of choosing, writing and sending your invitations. You will get tips and tricks on how to create your own unique, personalised stationery. But most of all you will see how to organise your stationery the stress free way and create that wow factor, whatever your budget.

Where do I start?

There is a huge variety of wedding stationery on the market. A good way to see what's on offer is to spend some time looking at different designs on the Internet. You may also want to browse mail order stationery catalogues, stationery shops or go to your local printer.

Most brides like to have matching thank you cards made when they place their stationery order. For a list of other stationery you may wish to order, see the Stationery Checklist later in this chapter.

Going with tradition

For a very traditional wedding the classic choice is good quality white or cream card, with wording on one side only in black or silver lettering. This always looks elegant and timeless.

A tissue overlay is placed over the invitation, which is then slipped inside an inner and then an outer envelope. This tradition originates from the days when a servant would remove the outer envelope and deliver the inner one by hand. The outer envelope has the full street address, whereas the inner one is addressed only with the person's name and is left unsealed. An inner envelope is not necessary for a less formal wedding although you can of course include one if you want to.

More contemporary options

If you want something more contemporary or unusual there is great scope for creativity. Browse large specialist paper shops for ideas. Here you will find paper of different weights, texture and colour. Look for accessories to customise the invitations once printed. These can include ribbon ties, wax seals, envelope linings or translucent overlays. Your printer will be able to tell you about using different fonts, colours or layouts.

Use your wedding stationery to carry through your theme. Link the day's events with matching bomboniere boxes, thank you cards, orders of service cards, place cards and menus. Many of these exquisite details are sure to become cherished mementos for close family in years to come.

One Stop Tip

Browsing stationery shops can be quite overwhelming. Bring a friend with a good eye for design for a second opinion.

Printing Methods

Engraving

Engraving dates back to the seventeenth century and is the most formal and expensive printing technique. The printer rolls ink on to a custom made engraved metal plate, which is wiped clean so the ink stays in the etched letters. They then press heavyweight paper onto the plate, leaving raised print on the front and an indentation on the back. Most printers let you keep the custom made copper plates as keepsakes.

Thermography

Thermography is currently the most popular choice for wedding invitations. It mimics engraving but is much cheaper. Powder is applied over the ink and then heated, which creates a raised lettering effect. Unlike engraving the reverse side of the paper stays smooth.

Lithography, Offset or Flat Printing

Offset printing, the technique used to print brochures and fliers, is one of your cheapest alternatives. An inked impression on a plate or rubber cylinder is transferred to paper to create flat lettering. This is one of the few methods which allow you to use multiple ink colours.

Digital Printing

Usually your least expensive option, digital printing works best on smooth or lightly textured paper. The image is sent to a high resolution digital printer without any loss of image quality. Colours are true to life and the image appears flat. The results are similar to those of offset printing.

Embossing

Embossing is most effective when used to accent an invitation with a monogram, motif, border or the return address on the envelope. A design is pressed into the back of the paper without the use of ink, creating a raised imprint. Although embossing is an additional cost, the elegant three dimensional effect may justify the extra expense.

Calligraphy

If you want beautifully hand-written envelopes consider hiring a professional calligrapher to address them for you. Alternatively you can create a similar effect at reduced cost by choosing a calligraphic font style which looks just like hand written calligraphy. Your stationer can print invitations and envelopes in the same calligraphic font so everything matches perfectly.

Personalised Stationery

If you want something completely unique, contact stationery companies who can create a design to your exact specifications. It's always worth looking at the designs they already have as these can often be altered slightly to suit your needs.

Bespoke stationery will of course cost more and delivery will take longer, so it's best to have an initial meeting with the designer about five months before your wedding. Agree on prices before the print run and get everything in writing so you are fully aware of what is included.

DIY Stationery

There is something very special about receiving a wedding invitation that has been hand made by the bride herself. Making your own stationery requires creativity and time, but it also gives you complete freedom of design and a real sense of satisfaction when you see your finished creation.

Get prepared

Leave yourself plenty of time – you do not want to be up late the night before your wedding day putting together orders of service. Gather together dress swatches and photos of the flowers you have selected, and browse invitations on the Web for ideas and inspiration.

Start shopping

Consider how you can use colour and texture to create something that captures your theme. Browse local paper shops for paper shot through with silk, metallic thread, seeds or petals. Look at different designs and textures like corrugated card, translucent paper and even pressed metal. Haberdasheries and bead shops are the places to look for ribbon, leather, cord and beads with which to customise your stationery.

Keep an eye out for craft shops where you can hunt down treasures such as feathers, shells, starfish, artificial flowers and pebbles at very reasonable prices. You could also include objects found in nature. Grasses, leaves, pine cones, pressed flowers or seed pods make lovely finishing touches.

Decide on a format

Think outside of the box – there's no reason to conform to the usual format. You might prefer to roll up your invitations and send them in cylinders or fabric covered boxes. Or try putting your invitations in transparent envelopes filled with bright confetti.

Credit yourself

Stationery that has been handcrafted by the bride is something to be treasured, so be sure to let your guests know. A simple note on the back saying 'made by ...' is all that is needed.

Print it

Once you have mocked up your design you will need to think about how it will be printed. A professional printer will always do a better job, but if you have a quality home printer you could go with this option instead. Experiment with different quality papers and print settings to give your text the best finish.

Put it together

Assembling your own stationery is a time consuming

task, so ask your bridesmaids or family round for a stationery making party. They will no doubt feel privileged that you asked for their help. Crack open the champagne, grab the double sided sticky tape and have some fun with it!

Stationery Checklist

There is more to consider than invitations and thank you cards. Much of the rest is optional, and how much stationery you want is a matter of personal choice. Here is a summary of all the stationery you might need to help you make your own mind up.

- ☐ Save the Date cards
- ☐ Bridal Shower invitations
- ☐ Stag Night invitations
- ☐ Hen Night invitations
- ☐ Kitchen Tea invitations
- ☐ Wedding Ceremony invitations
- ☐ Wedding Reception invitations
- ☐ After Party invitations
- ☐ RSVP cards, with or without stamped, addressed envelopes
- ☐ Directions and accommodation details
- ☐ Order of Service booklets
- ☐ Guest book
- ☐ Seating plan
- ☐ Table numbers
- ☐ Place cards
- ☐ Menus
- ☐ Bomboniere boxes
- ☐ Cake boxes
- ☐ Thank you cards

Invitation Ettiquette

Invitations are sent out from whoever is hosting the wedding. It is generally considered courteous to write each guest's name by hand. Typed or mail merged envelopes are usually regarded as too impersonal for an invitation to the most important celebration of your life, so envelopes should always be hand written. If you do not have good handwriting perhaps your groom, mother, mother-in-law or bridesmaid can assist with this task.

One invitation should be sent to each couple and one for each single guest. If you are inviting children, include their names on their parents' invitation. Anyone over the age of sixteen should receive a separate invitation. Be sure to include the host's return address on the envelope.

Invitations to the evening meal

If all guests are invited to both the ceremony and evening meal, you can print just one type of invitation. But what if you want more invited to the reception meal?

The answer is to print two different types of invitation – one to the ceremony and one to the reception. Guests invited to both events receive one of each. If you want to invite even more people to the after dinner party you will need to print a third type of invitation.

One Stop Tip

Remember to order a few extra invitations in case of spelling mistakes and other mishaps.

Including gift registry details

Wedding etiquette is constantly evolving. Strictly speaking it is not considered proper to include details on your gift registry with invitations, but over the last decade it has become increasingly common practice. If you are considering doing this think carefully about who is invited and how they will feel about it. Is anyone likely to take offence?

If most of your guests are computer literate, a good compromise is to list details of your gift registry on a wedding website. Just include your website's URL on invitations and let guests find the gift registry for themselves.

If in doubt, go with tradition. The safest approach is to ask your parents to field enquiries and your bridesmaids to tactfully spread the word as to where your gift list is registered. Most people will ask you or a member of your bridal party for your registry details anyway.

INVITING CHILDREN – OR NOT

If you want to invite children, include their names on their parents' invitation. Unless this has been specified parents should assume the invitation is for them alone. To make this clear you may choose to include a polite note on your invitations like 'We are sorry we are unable to accommodate children' or 'Much as we would like to invite all our friends' children, we are only able to accommodate the children of close family'. If you have arranged childcare, say something like 'Childminding facilities have been arranged for the duration of the reception'.

Invitation Enclosures

It is not essential to include reply cards with your invitations, but it often helps get a faster response. Include RSVP cards (stamping them is optional) or simply state the address and telephone number people need to respond to.

You can buy a pack of pre-printed RSVP cards from your stationers or have your own ones specially printed. The host's name and address can be pre-printed on the reply card envelope to make it easier for guests to respond.

You should also enclose directions and accommodation suggestions. Alternatively, if all your guests have internet access you can include directions and accommodation details on your wedding website. In this case your invitations should include a note saying something like 'For further details on arrangements please visit (URL)'.

PUTTING IT ALL TOGETHER

This is the traditional way to assemble invitations.

1. Put your reply card (if using) face-up under the flap of the reply card envelope.
2. Place the reply card and envelope, and any other enclosures face-up inside the invitation.
3. If you are using an inner envelope, insert the invitation face-up into it. The inner envelope should be left unsealed. (See 'Going with Tradition' at the beginning of this chapter for more details on inner envelopes.)
4. Put the inner envelop inside the outer one so the front of the inner envelope is visible.

Sending your invitations

Wedding invitations should be sent at least six to nine weeks before the big day. If your wedding falls on a holiday weekend, send them out much earlier. And if you are inviting friends and relatives from abroad, send them well in advance

– perhaps even six months to a year before the big day.

Don't forget to send invitations to your Mum, Dad, your groom's parents and the rest of the wedding party, even if they have already told you they will attend. Your officiant and their partner should be invited, and elderly relatives who are unable to attend will also appreciate an invitation.

Wedding Websites

Contrary to popular belief you need virtually no technical knowledge to set up your own wedding website – just use an online wedding website service. Putting a site together is as simple as filling out online forms and uploading a few photos. It costs only around US $100 for your own wedding website and it can be viewed for 18 months.

Benefits of a wedding website

Distributing information via a website is much cheaper than sending it by post. Each time you update your website, simply send out a mass email with a link to your site. Your website could include practical information such as:

- A map and directions
- Accommodation and car rental options for out of towners
- A link to your gift registry
- An online RSVP form
- A link to an online guide to your city
- Last minute updates on arrangements
- Weather forecast

…as well as fun items like:

- The story of how you met

- Childhood photographs of you and your groom
- Photos of the bridal party with a short summary of each person
- Photographs of the bridal shower, wedding and honeymoon
- Photos of you and your groom from the time you met up to the present day
- An online guestbook which any visitor to your site can browse or sign

Which website service?

One of the best and easiest to use wedding website services is www.weddings.myevent.com. Their service includes a free trial period, many different templates to choose from, online support and an impressive Flash intro. You can even choose a template which matches your wedding day colour scheme.

Wording your Invitations

The way you word your invitations will very much depend on the style and level of formality of your wedding. Some brides want traditional wording, whereas others prefer something more personalised or informal. Your choice of words will also depend on who is hosting the wedding. See the 'sample wordings' later in this chapter which can be adapted to suit your requirements.

Whatever you decide, include a minimum of the following information:

- Names of the hosts (traditionally the bride's parents)
- Names of the bride and groom, optionally including the groom's title
- Location of the ceremony

- Date, month and year of the ceremony
- Location of the reception
- RSVP address and reply date

You may also want to include:

- Dress code details
- Start time of the reception
- RSVP telephone number and / or email
- URL of the bride and groom's wedding website

YOUR PICTURE ON A POSTAGE STAMP

Several postal companies can create personalised postage stamps for you, featuring an engagement or wedding photograph. These are a wonderful way to commemorate your marriage and they can be sent out on your invitations or thank you cards. Prices are surprisingly reasonable. For further details visit your local post office.

Traditional Invitation Wording

Traditionally invitations are written in the third person – for example, 'Mr and Mrs Turner request the honour of your presence…' It is customary for the bride's name to appear before the groom's. The time and date should be written first followed by details of the venue. Titles such as Mr, Mrs or Dr should be used.

Invitations to religious ceremonies usually request 'the honour of your presence' whereas non-religious wedding invitations often ask for 'the pleasure of your company'. The below examples include both types of wording.

If hosted by the bride's parents:

Mr & Mrs Turner
Request the honour of your presence
at the marriage of their daughter
Chloe Elizabeth
to Jonathan Robert Belmont
son of
Mr & Mrs Belmont
on (date, month, year)
at (time)
St John's Church, Windsor
and afterwards at
The River Room, Ashfield House, Windsor

If hosted by the bride's parents (alternative):

Mr and Mrs Turner
Request the pleasure of the company of
(guest)
at the marriage of their daughter
Chloe Elizabeth
to
Jonathan Robert Belmont
son of
Mr & Mrs Belmont
on ...

If hosted by both sets of parents:

Mr & Mrs Turner
and
Mr & Mrs Belmont
request the pleasure of your company
at the marriage of their daughter
Chloe Elizabeth
to Jonathan Belmont
on ...

If hosted by the bride and groom and both sets of parents:

Mr & Mrs Turner
and their daughter
Chloe Elizabeth
together with
Mr & Mrs Belmont
and their son
Jonathan Robert
request the honour of your presence
at the wedding of
Chloe Elizabeth
and
Jonathan Robert
on ...

If hosted by the bride and groom:

> *Ms Chloe Elizabeth Turner*
> *and*
> *Mr Jonathan Robert Belmont*
> *request the pleasure of your company*
> *at their marriage*
> *on ...*

If jointly hosted by divorced parents:

> *Mr Turner*
> *and*
> *Mrs Thompson*
> *request the pleasure of your company*
> *at the marriage of their daughter*
> *Chloe Elizabeth Turner*
>
> *to*
> *Jonathan Robert Belmont*
> *son of*
> *Mr & Mrs Belmont*
> *on ...*

If hosted by a divorced parent and their spouse (the bride or groom's step parent):

Margaret & Nick Thompson
request the pleasure of your company
at the marriage of Margaret Thompson's daughter
Chloe Elizabeth Turner

to

Jonathan Robert Belmont
son of Mr & Mrs Belmont

on ...

If hosted by a single parent:

Mr Turner
requests the pleasure of your company
at the marriage of his daughter
Chloe Elizabeth

to

Jonathan Robert Belmont

on ...

If one parent is deceased and the wedding is hosted by the other:

In this instance the invitation should be written only from the surviving parent – there will be plenty of moments during the ceremony and speeches to honour their memory. This would read as follows:

> *Mr Turner*
> *requests the pleasure of your company*
> *at the marriage of his daughter*
> *Chloe Elizabeth*
> *to*
> *Jonathan Robert Belmont*
> *on ...*

However, if the event is being hosted by the bride and groom you may like to mention the deceased parent's name as follows:

> *Ms Chloe Elizabeth Turner*
> *daughter of Margaret Turner and the late Henry Turner*
> *and*
> *Mr Jonathan Robert Belmont*
> *son of Mr and Mrs Belmont*
> *request the pleasure of your company*
> *at their marriage*
> *on ...*

Contemporary Invitation Wording

More modern wording allows some scope to convey the way you feel about your marriage. You could for example 'warmly invite' your guests to join you on the 'joyful occasion' of your wedding. Parents hosting the wedding may want to convey their happiness by saying they are 'proud to invite' guests to the festivities. You can even combine traditional phrases with more modern ones. See the following sample wordings for inspiration.

If hosted by the bride and groom:

Chloe Elizabeth Turner
and
Jonathan Robert Belmont
invite
(guest)
to share in their joy
as they exchange marriage vows
at
St John's Church, Windsor
on (date)
at (time)
and afterwards at
The River Room, Ashfield House, Windsor

If hosted by the bride and groom (alternate):

Chloe Elizabeth Turner
and
Jonathan Robert Belmont
warmly invite
(guest)
to join them on the joyful occasion of their marriage
at ...

If hosted by the bride's parents:

> *Mr and Mrs Turner*
> *are proud to invite*
> *(guest)*
> *to share in their joy*
> *at the marriage of their daughter*
> *Chloe Elizabeth*
> *to*
> *Jonathan Robert Belmont*
> *at ...*

Reply Cards

Use wording which simply allows guests to delete as appropriate, as follows:

> _____
>
> *are pleased to attend / are regretfully unable to attend*
> *the marriage of*
> *your daughter, Chloe Elizabeth, to*
> *Mr. Jonathan Robert Belmont*
> *On (date, month, year)*
>
> *Special dietary requirements (if applicable):*
>
> _____
>
> *Please RSVP by (date)*

Pre-Wedding Stationery

You may also wish to order stationery for any pre-wedding parties and events you are planning. This is very much a matter of personal choice – whilst some brides like to invite guests formally, others prefer to just ring round or email.

Engagement party invitations

Traditionally the bride's parents host the engagement party, but where this is not possible the groom's parents host it. If you want to distribute formal invitations they can be worded as follows:

Mr. and Mrs. Turner
request the pleasure of your company
at a dinner in honour of
Miss Chloe Elizabeth and Mr Jonathan Robert Belmont
on
(Day and date)
at
(Time)
(Full address)
RSVP

or

> *Miss Chloe Elizabeth Turner*
> *and*
> *Mr Jonathan Robert Belmont*
> *request the pleasure of your company at a party in their honour*
> *on*
> *(Day and date)*
> *at*
> *(Time)*
> *(Full address)*
> *RSVP*

'Save the Date' cards

If you want to send 'Save the Date' cards, they can be worded as follows:

> *Please save the date of*
> *(day and date)*
> *for the wedding of*
> *Miss Chloe Elizabeth Turner*
> *to*
> *Mr Jonathan Robert Belmont*
>
> *Mr and Mrs Turner*

Bridal shower invitations

The bridal shower takes place around a month before your wedding and is usually thrown by your chief bridesmaid.

If you want to have a gift theme to guide your guests, such as linen or kitchenware, this can be mentioned in the invitation. Otherwise your chief bridesmaid may wish to tell those invited where your wedding gift list is registered so friends can buy you some of the smaller items. This is a good way to limit the likelihood of getting duplicate gifts and ensure every present is something you really want or need.

If you are sending formal invitations they can be worded as follows:

> *(Host friend's Christian name and surname)*
> *requests the pleasure of your company*
> *at a Bridal Shower*
> *in honour of*
> *Chloe Turner*
> *on*
> *(Day and date)*
> *at*
> *(Time)*
> *(Full address)*

Rehearsal Dinner Invitations

The rehearsal dinner, usually held the night before the wedding, is traditionally hosted by the groom's parents. Only the bridal party and occasionally out of town guests are invited. Invitations are not necessary but if you do want to send them they should complement, but not compete with, your wedding invitations. One way of wording them is:

Mr. and Mrs. Belmont
request the pleasure of your company
at a rehearsal dinner
in honour of
Chloe and Jonathan
on
(date, month, year)
at
(Time)
(Full address)

Orders of Service

The Order of Service is a small booklet distributed by the groomsmen to guests as they arrive. It records the sequence of events in the marriage ceremony, details of any music that is played and poems or bible passages that are read. The booklets help guests follow events as they unfold and, in a religious ceremony, means they don't have to juggle hymn books.

Orders of Service can be used at both religious and non religious weddings. The wording will depend on the sequence of events, which is slightly different for each ceremony. Your minister or celebrant will be your best source of advice. They can guide you on the correct wording for each part of the ceremony as well as the suitability of any poems or readings you have chosen. If you want to honour a deceased close relative, you can include a short poem or prayer dedicated to them in your Orders of Service.

Traditional Layout

The traditional booklet is a simple piece of A4 card folded in half with paper inserts. The front cover usually presents the details of the marriage ceremony including the full names of the bride and groom, date and location. Sometimes a short poem or the names of the bridal party are included on the first page. After this each section of the ceremony is listed in order.

Sample Order of Service cover wording

St John's Church,
Windsor

The marriage of
Chloe Elizabeth Turner
&
Jonathan Robert Belmont

(date, time)

Alternative Layouts

Order of Service booklets do not need to be boring – there's plenty of opportunity to personalise them. Perhaps you want them to match your invitations or continue your colour scheme? You might choose a square format rather than the traditional A4 dimensions or ask an artistic friend to draw a picture of the church for the front cover.

You can use ribbons, beads or shells to add texture and dimension and coordinate them with the rest of your stationery. Just make sure to check the final design and contents with your celebrant before you have them printed.

When working out how many booklets need to be printed, remember to include the officiant and choir in your calculations. Some couples prefer to share a booklet so you only need to print copies for about three quarters of your guests.

Orders of Service are often kept as mementos, so you may find they all disappear with your guests at the end of the ceremony! Print several extras for yourself so you can save your own keepsakes of the day, and perhaps even hand them on to future generations.

Sample of an Order of Service

Entrance of the Bride: 'Shine'

Introduction and Welcome

Opening Reading by Beatrice Wilson:
Extract from 'The Voice of the Master' by Kahlil Gibran

Prayer

Declaration of Freedom

Bible Reading by Stephen Gibson:
Psalm I, The Book of Psalms

Hymn:
Make Me a Channel of Your Peace
(hymn text goes here)

Vows

Address

Reading by Rev Martin O'Sullivan:
Extract from 'The Broken Wings' by Kahlil Gibran

Cherokee Prayer, read by Paula Saunders

Signing of the Register

Presentation of the Bride and Groom

Recessional: 'Higher and Higher'

Reception Stationery

Seating Plan

Position a seating plan near the entrance to your reception venue to help guests quickly and easily find their way to their seats. A piece of card at least A3 in size should be printed with lists of your guests names under each table number.

For a larger wedding it may be necessary to assist your guests by also displaying a birds' eye view of the location of each table within the room. You could also station a couple of groomsmen at the door to direct guests to their seats.

Table numbers

Table numbers are a practical way of indicating where your guests should sit. Paint them on the side of terracotta pots containing your flowers, mount them in silver frames or write them on thick card in elegant calligraphy.

Alternatively, why not give your tables names? You could name each one after a special place you enjoyed spending time, the word 'love' in different languages or even after the names you have short listed for your future children. They are a great way to incorporate your theme, so if you are marrying on a tropical island you might want to name them after the island's wildlife or beaches.

Place card ideas

Place cards are useful to indicate exactly where your guests should sit. They may be written by hand or professionally printed. Here are some ideas:

- Use black ink to write your guests' names in calligraphy on pieces of card, tucking each one into a folded white linen napkin.
- Small silver or carved wooden frames make lovely favours and can double up as place cards.
- Tie two or three indoor sparklers with ribbon and a small tag bearing your guest's name.
- For place cards that double as bombonieres, tie name tags onto small jars of delicious homemade jam.
- Ice gingerbread men with each guest's name.

Favours

Wedding favours, also known as bombonieres, are a special thank you to your guests for sharing your day. They allow your friends and family to take home a little bit of the magic of your wedding day, and often become treasured keepsakes for many years to come.

The tradition of giving wedding favours has long been

popular. Seventeenth century high society guests were given scarves, gloves, a small item of jewellery or semi-precious stones. As sugar became increasingly available favours evolved into the familiar five sugared almonds which represent health, wealth, happiness, long life and fertility.

These days favours can be whatever your heart desires. Purchase ready-made ones from a wedding shop, buy the containers and fillings separately and assemble them yourself, or make your own boxes or bags from scratch and fill them with whatever you wish.

Favour Ideas

- Mini port, spirit or champagne bottles with labels bearing your wedding details
- Small bottles of home blended aromatherapy oil tied with ribbon
- CDs featuring music from your wedding
- Boxes of luxury chocolates tied with braided gold cord or ribbon
- Pretty beaded votive holders
- Home-made chocolate chip cookies or brownies boxed and tied with ribbon

One Stop Tip

Instead of printing up place cards, why not prepare an overall seating plan and let guests mix it up within each table?

Cost Saving Tips for your Stationery

- Go minimalist – a simple, classic invitation looks stylish and costs less than an elaborate one.

- Instead of enclosing a stamped addressed reply card, simply print 'RSVP to' followed by your address and telephone number.
- Create your own home-made invitations on your computer. If you have a good printer, print them out at home on good quality paper.
- Buy plain, brightly coloured little paper bags or boxes and invite your bridesmaids round for a favour-making party. Decorate them with ribbon, a shell, feather or strand of beads and fill them with inexpensive sweets.
- Sew little pouches from organza, tie them with satin ribbon and fill them with sweets – a metre of organza costs little but goes a long way.
- Buy small cactuses or herbs from a gardening centre and re-pot them in terracotta containers, tying a ribbon around each one.
- Make edible place cards which double as favours (see 'Place Card Ideas').
- If you do without favours completely, will anyone actually notice? Think of all the weddings you have been to in the last three years and see if you can remember what the favours looked like – and if you remembered to take one home!

One Stop Review

- ☐ Find inspiration by browsing stationery designs on the Internet or in catalogues.
- ☐ Choose an invitation design and printing method which captures your day's tone, level of formality and colour scheme.
- ☐ Personalise your invitations with translucent overlays, embossing, calligraphy or ribbon.

☐ Continue your design in your place cards, thank you cards and other stationery.

☐ Use every opportunity to personalise your day, from illustrated Orders of Service to monogrammed place cards.

Notes

Notes

Transport

For the most important journey of your life you'll want a ride that gets you there in style. This chapter shows you how to choose transport that expresses your theme and makes a statement about who you are as a couple. It will also guide you through some of the more practical issues of vehicle hire, so you can rest assured that whatever you choose it will be comfortable, affordable and most importantly, get you to the church on time!

Where do I Start?

Use the style of the occasion as your starting point. A sophisticated event might call for a Bentley or Daimler, or a stretched limo for a touch of Hollywood glamour. Couples marrying on the beach however might prefer to bring a sense of adventure to their day by arriving by dune buggy or speed boat.

Match the location

Look for inspiration in your location. That black cab could be just the thing once decorated if you're a Londoner – and why not have a bright red double-decker bus transfer guests to the reception? On the other hand a wedding in the countryside could call for a romantic horse drawn carriage, vintage Rolls Royce – or even a tractor!

Express your personality

Another approach is to take your personality as the cue. If you're a James Bond fan hire a racy Aston Martin, or add an American retro vibe with a vintage Chevrolet. If you're known for your love affair with your VW beetle, why not dress it up in ribbons and drive it to your ceremony?

Colour coordinate

Check your vehicle's colour doesn't clash with your bouquet. Your photographer is sure to take some shots as you arrive, and the more colour coordinated everything is the better it will look in your photos. A ribbon for the bonnet in your wedding's theme colour adds a lovely finishing touch.

One Stop Tip

You can either arrange separate transport for your mum and bridesmaids or ask your chauffeur to do two trips. The bride, of course, should be the last to arrive at the ceremony.

Plan for your gown

Whichever mode of transport you choose, make sure there's enough room to comfortably accommodate your dress so it doesn't get crushed. A sports car is fine if you're wearing something simple, but for a full gown a stretched limousine is a better choice.

Or just go by foot

If the ceremony and reception venue are close to your home, why not go by foot? A bride walking to her wedding with her father or from it with her groom is a rare and beautiful sight, and you will get lots of congratulations and compliments from passers by. Just make sure you've worn in your shoes!

> ### DECORATING YOUR RIDE
>
> Wedding car hire companies often decorate the vehicle as part of their service. However if a friend is chauffeuring you, ask someone in your bridal party to spruce up the car with ribbons, balloons, a 'just married' sign, streamers or a few flowers. Attaching a ribbon to the car bonnet can be a little fiddly, so choose someone handy and leave spare time in your schedule.

Cost Saving Tips for your Transport

- Ask a friend with an attractive or unique car to act as chauffeur for the day.
- Hiring a limousine on a day other than a Saturday is often cheaper.
- If the ceremony is close to your house and the reception venue, consider hiring one driver who can make multiple trips to pick up bridesmaids and family.
- Hire a limousine without the mini-bar and TV to save money – you will be too excited to use them anyway.
- If your reception and ceremony venues are close to each other, a bicycle made for two can be a romantic, fun and cost effective way to arrive at your reception. Tie streamers to the handlebars and attach a 'Just Married' helium-filled balloon to the back.

One Stop Tip

Traditionally the bride travels to the wedding with her father, the bride's mother goes with the bridesmaids and the groom with his best man.

Guaranteeing a Smooth Ride

If hiring, make sure you examine the car *in person* before booking or paying a deposit. Photos in leaflets or on a website are always taken from the best angle, and will not show dents or a scruffy interior.

Booking your Transport

When booking your vehicle, give the chauffeur a checklist including all pick-up and drop off locations, timings, maps and phone numbers. The last thing you want on your wedding day is to find out your chauffeur is lost. Give passengers the directions too in case the driver misplaces the information.

Bring out the bubbly

Enjoy a celebratory drink as you travel from the ceremony to the reception. Ask a member of your bridal party to arrange for a bottle of Champagne to be chilling on ice in the car.

Get it in writing

Get a contract, with all the details of the rental agreement in writing. It should include costs, timings and pick up and drop off locations.

Confirm your booking

Ring to confirm your transport hire one week before the

big day so you don't find it's been double booked. If it has, it's time to get out that contract.

Bring your luggage

Arrange for your luggage to be taken to your hotel – or, if you're leaving for your honeymoon straight after the wedding, to the reception venue. The best man traditionally arranges this, so make sure he knows what to do well before the big day.

Make sure it's clean

Borrowing a car from a friend? Then arrange for it to be valeted the day before your wedding, and check the tank is full!

Make arrangements for your guests

How will your guests get from your ceremony to the reception? Organising a courtesy bus transfer is a thoughtful gesture if your budget allows it, but by no means a necessity. Just be sure to give your guests advance notice of their transport options. Give them detailed maps and directions if there's any chance they could get lost.

CHOOSING A RELIABLE CAR HIRE SERVICE

By all means shop around, but don't base your decision purely on price. A reliable company with well maintained, smart looking cars is sure to cost more – but it's worth paying the extra. Ask recently married friends for recommendations or look for a company which owns its own fleet, as these tend to maintain their cars to a higher standard than those which rent their vehicles from other companies. Visit the company yourself, examine its vehicles carefully inside and out and confirm that the drivers are courteous and will be dressed appropriately.

One Stop Review

- ☐ Choose a vehicle that is in keeping with the style of your day.
- ☐ Make sure it compliments the location, expresses your personality and matches your colour scheme as much as possible.
- ☐ Check it is large enough to comfortably accommodate your dress without crushing it.
- ☐ Find a reliable car hire company, get your booking in writing and ring to confirm it a week before your wedding.
- ☐ Decorate your ride with helium balloons, streamers, ribbon and flowers.

Notes

Notes

Flowers

From the bridal garlands of ancient Rome to the Victorians' use of floral symbolism to pass on secret messages, the language of flowers has always been a bride's most eloquent and beautiful form of self expression. This chapter will show how you, too, can mark every stage of your wedding with unique, enchanting arrangements.

Discover step by step how to use flowers to express your personality, theme and the feel of your wedding day. Find out how to choose a bouquet which flatters your gown, and get tips on how to use flowers to highlight focal points at your ceremony and reception.

With a little creative thinking, every bride can afford exquisite floral arrangements. Use the advice in this chapter and you'll be surprised just how far your budget will stretch.

Where do I Start?

Begin by thinking about the mood and feel you want to create. This will be guided by your overall wedding theme and colour scheme.

Ask yourself, do you want traditional arrangements or more modern ones? Bold, bright flowers or pretty, feminine blooms? Flick through magazines and browse the internet for inspiration. Look for arrangements that appeal to you and save pictures of them in an Ideas Folder. You can take this along when you interview florists to give them an idea of the look you want them to create.

Express yourself

The most important thing in your choice is not the 'official' meanings of your flowers, but what they mean to you personally. So choose blooms that you feel best express who you are as an individual. The romantic bride with a traditional sense of style might choose a trailing bouquet of classic roses or blowsy pink peonies. Pink or yellow frangipanis may appeal to someone with a love of the exotic, whereas brightly coloured gerberas or sunflowers could be the choice of an original, spirited bride to express joyfulness and a sense of fun.

Complimentary colours

Colour associations can also transform the meaning and association of a flower. For example white phalaenopsis orchids seem stylish and sophisticated, whereas bright pink ones look lush, sensual and tropical.

Some brides take their cue for flowers from the colour of their bridesmaid dresses, whilst others choose their flowers first and then find dresses to coordinate. You may decide to go to your florist with just a colour or dress fabric swatch and see what they can come up with.

Think outside of the box when choosing a colour scheme. Contrasting two different colours, like turquoise bridesmaids dresses with gold flowers, can be very effective. This is because they are at opposite ends of the colour wheel.

A Flower for all seasons

Theming your wedding around a season? Then use this as your starting point. An **autumn** wedding can be enhanced with rich toned flowers in crimson and amber with deep jade-green foliage. **Winter** brides might decorate tables with potted flowers, such as poinsettias, traditionally displayed at Christmas in Europe, or red roses, mistletoe, holly and ivy.

Springtime flowers in fresh pastel shades can be used to create a romantic, nostalgic feel. Think soft lilacs, dusky pinks and pea green. Bulb flowers like daffodils and tulips work well, as do sweet scented hyacinths and freesias.

Summer is the season for bold, strong colours so create an exotic look with bright tropical blooms. Alternatively go for the country cottage garden look with full-blooming roses and meadow inspired loose, casual arrangements.

Saying It With Flowers

Floral symbolism reached its peak in the Victorian age when meanings were assigned to each flower to convey different sentiments. Lovers would send specific flowers to each other to convey secret messages. If you would like your wedding flowers to communicate the way you feel about your beloved, take a look at each flower's meaning before you make your choice.

Apple Blossom	Good fortune
Baby's Breath	Pure Heart
Carnation	Distinction
Chrysanthemum	Friendship
Daffodil	Joy
Daisy	Loyalty

Forget-me-not	True Love
Gardenia	Joy
Gladiolus	Generosity
Heather	Admiration and Protection
Iris	Wisdom
Ivy	Fidelity, wedded love
Lavender	Devotion
Lily	Happiness
Lily of the Valley	Return of happiness
Magnolia	Nobility, dignity
Mint	Prosperity
Myrtle	Love
Orange Blossom	Fertility
Orchid	Rare beauty
Peony	Happiness
Red Chrysanthemum	Sharing
Rose	Love and purity
Rosemary	Fidelity and remembrance
Thyme	Courage, strength
Violet	Faithfulness
White Lilac	Innocence

The Bridal Bouquet

The bouquet has always been a bride's most coveted accessory. It takes centre stage from the moment you walk down the aisle, captivating your guests as a symbol of beauty and abundance right until it's thrown to the single ladies at the end of the night.

Your bouquet should complete, rather than compete with, your bridal gown. A large arrangement can overwhelm a simple dress whereas a small posy might be hidden against a full-skirted ball gown. Take a photo or sketch of your gown to your florist so you can be sure that your bouquet will compliment it. The following table will give you some guidelines.

Gown style	Suits
Traditional full skirted	Large shower bouquet of flowers such as roses or orchids
Slim fitting gown	Small bouquet, posy or long shower style
Princess line	Teardrop or trailing bouquet
Simple dress	Extravagant bouquet
Detailed dress	Simple, medium sized bouquet or arm sheaf
Light, floaty fabric	Bouquet of small, delicate flowers like lily-of-the-valley
Heavy fabric like velvet or satin	Rich, strong coloured flowers or simple, sculptural blooms like white arum lilies or gardenias

Your bouquet should also reflect the style, theme, location and formality of your ceremony. A casual posy of blooms can look pretty at a country wedding, but a church ceremony might call for something more dramatic like a trailing arrangement.

You will usually find that hand-tied posies or cascade bouquets work well in outdoor locations where they complement and echo the natural environment. However a more structured arrangement like a biedermeier will suit the avant-garde bride marrying in a chic city location.

Bouquet Shapes Explained

Posy

The **natural stem** or **hand tied** posy is a bouquet of long stemmed flowers tied together with a ribbon. Stems are bluntly cut for that fresh, just picked look and the bouquet looks pretty and informal. Fully wired posies look quite different however, as they have had the stems removed and replaced with florists' wire. This gives the bouquet a more neat, polished look.

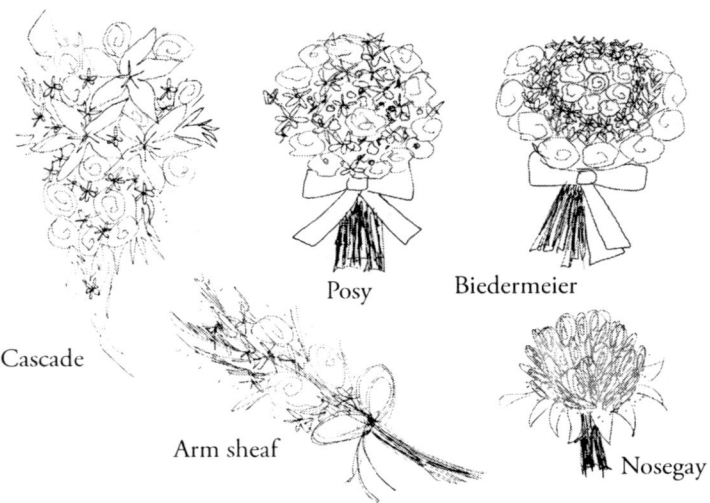

Cascade

Posy

Biedermeier

Arm sheaf

Nosegay

Biedermeier

The Biedermeier is a variation on the posy where different coloured flowers are arranged in concentric circles. This tightly-structured bouquet heralds from the 1800s, but its contrasting colours and dramatic symmetry make it an increasingly popular choice for stylish modern brides looking for something unusual.

Nosegay

This is a small posy of flowers and occasionally sprigs of herbs or berries, tied or wired together. They are a popular choice for flower girls and bridesmaids.

Arm Sheaf

As its name suggests this bouquet is cradled in one arm. It is a good choice for brides who want a natural look, but prefer something larger and more dramatic than a posy.

Cascade or Shower

Long stemmed flowers and greenery which fall in a graceful waterfall shape. The sweeping, elegant line of these longer style bouquets can be more flattering to the figure than the plump, round shape of a posy. They compliment elaborate or vintage gowns beautifully.

One Stop Tip

Taller brides can carry off a large, ornamental bouquet, whereas a smaller bouquet is usually more flattering for the petite bride.

Buttonholes and Corsages

Buttonholes and corsages are a great way to link the entire wedding party, publicly singling out each person as extra-special. Your groom's buttonhole can be taken from a flower in your bouquet, whilst the best man and groomsmen may prefer to wear a flower featured in your bridesmaids' bouquets. Consider ordering buttonholes and corsages for parents, grandparents and other close family, who will no doubt be proud to be included.

Flowers for Hair

For a fresh, pretty look ask your florist to wire some fresh flowers for you and your bridesmaids to wear in your hair. Decorating your hair with flowers looks particularly lovely at an outdoor or countryside wedding, and it's perfect for child attendants and flower girls.

HOT WEATHER ALERT

Warm weather causes some flowers to wilt, so choose ones that can take the heat like roses. Wired bouquets fare better in hot weather as the heat of a bride's hands can cause the blooms of a natural stem posy to go limp.

Ceremony Flowers

Strategically placed throughout your venue, flowers bring colour and life to your space. They create a sense of occasion, and help to highlight the site of your marriage as special and significant. You may want to use some of the following techniques to decorate your venue.

Define your space

If you are marrying in an outdoor location like a garden or golf course it is important to visually define the boundaries of your ceremony. You can do this with scattered petals down the aisle, a decorated archway positioned at the front, or floral arrangements lining the aisle on each pew end or seat.

Welcome guests

Floral arrangements at the entrance of your ceremony venue will make your guests feel welcome and create an attractive area to have photographs taken later. If there are steps, try framing the walk up to the entrance with inexpensive potted flowers on alternate steps. Potted topiary trees can be hired to frame the entrance. Ask your florist to tuck a few blooms into the foliage so they look like flowering shrubs.

Create a focal point

Arrangements at the front of your venue where you and your groom stand will emphasize the focal point for your marriage ceremony. To decorate the table used for signing the registry, simply ask your bridesmaids to rest their bouquets here for the duration of the ceremony. You may also wish to highlight this space with floral arrangements mounted on pedestals.

Reuse your flowers

Get the most of out of your flowers. Ask a friend to transport them to your reception venue so you can enjoy them all over again. Decide whether you want to do this at the outset and discuss it with your florist, as this will influence the types of decorations you choose and how they are made. Pedestal arrangements can be reused to frame the entrance, pew ends to line pathways and bouquets can serve as table centrepieces.

Use floral confetti

If you are marrying outdoors, rose petals can be used as a pretty and ecological alternative to confetti. Ask your florist for fresh petals from the flower farm's 'seconds' – a large bag of blooms is inexpensive but goes a long way. Get a friend to detach the petals from the fresh blooms just before the ceremony. They can be put into small wicker baskets, available at low cost from any craft shop, or simple card cones. Your groomsmen can give one to each guest framing the aisle.

Cost Saving Tips for your Flowers

- The first thing guests see are the bouquets and ceremony venue flowers, so focus your funds on these.
- If you're marrying in church find out if another wedding is taking place the same day – you may be able to share the cost of flowers and halve your costs. Choose a neutral tone like white or cream so it coordinates with both colour schemes.
- Let your florist know if you are on a tight budget and encourage them to get creative. Costs can be cut substantially by using flowers which are in season and dressing them with plenty of greenery. You may find you have enough money for table arrangements after all.
- Ask your reception venue staff if they have any table decorations of their own. Often they will let you use these for free, and they can always be dressed up with flowers or candles.
- Do you have your heart set on an expensive flower? Then feature it in your bouquets only and mix it up with less expensive blooms.

> ## One Stop Tip
> Some floral presentation companies specialise in preserving bridal bouquets. If you want your bouquet preserved, ask your florist to make up a second, simpler bouquet to throw to your friends at the end of the night.

Reception Flowers

You can use flowers to create almost any look or feel you like. For visual continuity however the flowers at your reception should be similar to those used at the ceremony.

Create focal points

Dressing the whole room with similar arrangements can look bland. Flowers are more effective when used to emphasise focal points. One of these is the venue's entrance, which can be strikingly framed with two pedestal arrangements or topiaries. You may want to have topiaries, pedestal arrangements or flowered arches from your ceremony transported and reused at your reception. The top table is also an area which you can mark out as extra special with more elaborate table displays. As for the cake table, a simple way to dress this is to ask your bridesmaids to rest their bouquets there during the meal.

Choose take-away arrangements

Flowers undoubtedly add something special to a room, but many brides feel it's a shame only to enjoy them for one day. If you want to make them last, ask your florist to create table centrepieces from several separate clusters of flowers. This way each couple can take one bunch home and they can be enjoyed for longer.

Use live flowering plants

If your budget does not stretch to table centrepieces, consider buying live flowering plants from a gardening centre. You can replant them in inexpensive terracotta pots for a pretty cottage garden look. Green fingered brides might even like to grow their own flowers from scratch. This is a great way to personalise your reception with a contribution to be really proud of. When the day is over you can give away home grown flowers as thank you gifts to friends and family.

Decorate with petals

Scatter fresh rose petals onto tables for a fresh, summery feel. This can create quite a dramatic look at little cost. Freeze-dried petals will also work but they will not look as fresh and are more expensive. Your florist will be able to get you a large bag of fresh roses at low cost from a flower farm's 'seconds'. You could ask a friend to detach the petals and sprinkle them across your reception tables before guests enter. For non-floral table decoration ideas, please see the Reception chapter.

Wedding Flower Checklist

- ☐ Bridal bouquet
- ☐ Bridesmaid bouquets
- ☐ Buttonholes
- ☐ Corsages
- ☐ Pew ends
- ☐ Flowers at the ceremony entrance
- ☐ Floral arch
- ☐ Registry table flowers
- ☐ Flowers for the altar
- ☐ Petal confetti
- ☐ Petals for the aisle

- ☐ Table arrangements
- ☐ Pedestals at reception entrance
- ☐ Fresh flowers for your wedding cake

Finding a Florist

Word of mouth is often the best way to find a florist, so ask for recommendations from friends whose wedding flowers you liked. Keep an eye out for local florists with interesting and original shop displays. Also search wedding magazines and the Internet for appealing arrangements.

Once you have a shortlist of three or four florists, make appointments with each of them. Be open about your budget from the start so they know what they have to work with. To bring them closer to your thinking show them pictures of arrangements which you particularly like, photos of your venue and swatches of fabric from your wedding gown and brides-maids' dresses.

Tell them about the look you want to create, ask for ideas and view some examples of their work. The best florist for you will not necessarily be the most expensive or fashionable, so trust your intuition and choose someone whose work you love.

Questions for your florist

- ☐ Can you see photographs from other weddings they have worked on?
- ☐ Will they personally be arranging your flowers, or will it be another member of their team?
- ☐ Which flowers will be in season when you get married?
- ☐ Do they have any other weddings booked on the same day?
- ☐ Will they arrange your flowers on site, or just organise for them to be delivered?

☐ When do you need to pay them the deposit and final balance?

One Stop Review

☐ Express yourself with flowers that reflect your personality.

☐ Walk down the aisle with a stunning bouquet that flatters the shape of your gown.

☐ Involve loved ones by giving them buttonholes or corsages to wear.

☐ Choose a florist whose work you love, and be honest about your budget from the start.

☐ Use flowers to highlight the focal points of your ceremony and reception.

Notes

Notes

The Ceremony

Marriage is an ancient ritual shared by almost every culture and society throughout history. This public declaration conveys your profound commitment to each other and celebrates one of the most enduring expressions of human love. Your marriage ceremony will be a deeply significant moment for you both, as it marks the start of the new life you are embarking on together.

There are no two people alike and so no two marriage ceremonies will be quite the same. This chapter will show you how to make yours a unique expression of your own personalities, the love you share and the special qualities you bring together in your partnership.

What Sort of Ceremony?

Your decision on whether to have a civil or religious ceremony will ultimately depend on your own personal beliefs and those of your groom. It is also, however, wise to be sensitive to the wishes and religious beliefs of your families. You might want to bear the following points in mind when exploring the possibilities.

Religious	Civil
Even if you don't want to marry in a place of worship you can still have a religious ceremony as many ministers of religion are now happy to conduct marriage ceremonies outside of religious buildings. You could marry in a place of natural beauty such as a rose garden, beach or rainforest. Services in such locations can seem less formal and often underplay religious dogma, instead emphasising the spiritual aspect of marriage. This can be a good compromise if you and your groom share a belief in God but do not consider yourselves religious, or where only one of you is religious. The idea of marrying outdoors can also appeal to those with strong spiritual or New Age beliefs.	A civil ceremony allows you complete freedom of choice: you select the words, music and exactly how the ceremony is to be conducted. So long as you include the legal wording from the Marriage Act the format and wording of the service is pretty much up to you. Your celebrant can help you plan and write your own vows as well as offering guidance on how to personalise the ceremony. You may like to include poems, music or readings. Many celebrants will be only too happy to incorporate your own beliefs and any rituals that are particularly meaningful to you. These could include a unity candle or hand-fasting ritual, spiritual wording or even blessings.

One Stop Tip

If you're not a regular church goer you can still get married in church. Many churches are available for weddings even if you're not a member of that denomination.

Choosing your Officiant

Whether you're having a civil or religious marriage, it's vital that you feel completely comfortable with the person who will be marrying you. Apart from their role on your big day they will also guide you through the legal requirements and documentation in the lead-up to your wedding, so it's important to choose someone you can trust.

If you're marrying in church you will probably not have much choice as to which officiant marries you. However it's still wise to make sure you are comfortable with them. If not, find out if you can meet the other ministers who work there – or choose another church!

Where do I Start?

Begin by telephoning a few officiants so you get an idea of who you feel most comfortable with. Some even have websites or ads in wedding magazines which tell you a little about them and show you a photograph of what they look like.

When you are down to two or three favourites, call them and arrange a time to meet and ask questions. Ultimately you should choose someone articulate who puts you at ease whom you can easily imagine presiding over your marriage.

Questions for your Officiant

- ☐ Are they able to travel to your ceremony location?
- ☐ Are they happy to make changes to the service?
- ☐ What will they wear?
- ☐ Are there restrictions if you and your fiancé are of different faiths?
- ☐ Will they marry you if you are previously divorced?

Questions for Yourself

- ☐ Does this person put you at ease?
- ☐ Do you feel you and your groom would be the centre of the ceremony rather than the officiant?
- ☐ Are they asking the right questions to find out what sort of ceremony you want?
- ☐ Is the officiant friendly and personable?
- ☐ Do they make you feel comfortable asking questions, however simple?
- ☐ Do they seem enthusiastic, or do they just see your wedding as just another job?
- ☐ Were they able to answer your questions confidently?
- ☐ Did they offer any ideas or suggestions?
- ☐ How strong are their public speaking skills?
- ☐ Is this someone you feel you would like to keep in touch with after your wedding?

Choosing your Ceremony Venue

The location you choose for your ceremony will influence the feel of your wedding more than almost anything else, so use this opportunity to choose an enchanting spot that is a worthy backdrop to your marriage. Also consider where you are permitted to marry according your country's laws (see the Regional Variations box earlier in this chapter).

You could choose a stunning waterfront spot, grand historic house, private chapel, church or winery. Alternatively the manicured lawns of award-winning gardens might make a picturesque setting. Or marry on a mountaintop, as the sun sets over rolling hills which stretch out to the distant ocean.

One Stop Tip

Marrying for the second time? Many ministers do not have a problem marrying divorcees so a church wedding is still an option.

You could even opt for a romantic rainforest retreat, where your guests can soak up the natural scenery and unwind with relaxing spa treatments. And if you have already set your heart on a place for your reception, look out for somewhere nearby to hold your ceremony like a pretty gazebo or rose garden in the venue's grounds.

An increasingly popular trend is what's known as the destination wedding. Here the whole wedding party travels to a stunning wedding location to enjoy a long weekend of sun, fun and feasting.

Although more expensive for you and your guests, escaping to an exotic island can be a wonderful and memorable treat for smaller, more intimate gatherings. Some island hotels employ staff dedicated entirely to coordinating such weddings, so despite the distance the planning might be easier than you think.

Ceremony Venue Checklist

- ☐ Can it comfortably accommodate all your guests?
- ☐ How far is it from the reception venue?
- ☐ Do you get a good feeling about this place?
- ☐ Is there sufficient parking?
- ☐ Is there disabled access?
- ☐ Is there space for a receiving line if you want one?
- ☐ How much does it cost to hire the venue?
- ☐ If it's outdoors, what are the wet weather alternatives?
- ☐ Can you choose your own officiant?
- ☐ Does the venue permit filming and photography?

Creating Ambience

Ambience is the special atmosphere or mood created by a particular environment – that elusive magic ingredient that adds character and makes some ceremonies unforgettable. Whether you want your ceremony to inspire a sense of joy and fun or an aura of romance and intimacy, you will need to engage every one of the five senses.

Sight

The look of your ceremony venue and the view from it will play a large part in the type of ambience you create. Think about the time of day you choose – a beach ceremony will have a different feeling (and temperature) at midday than at sunset. Here are some ideas that will help you achieve your desired look.

Decoration

Think about how you can use colour and form to add atmosphere. Depending on the time of day you may wish to light candles, use subdued lighting or string fairy lights through the trees. Chair covers can add a special touch, and you may want to hire topiary trees or exotic plants for the entrance.

COLOUR THERAPY

Pick your wedding colour with the mood in mind:
Red – for courage, strength and passion
Yellow – for wisdom and harmony
Brown – for healing and the home
Green – for health, prosperity, luck, fertility and beauty
Dark Blue – for a safe journey and longevity
Light Blue – for understanding and patience
Pink – for romance, honour, partnership and happiness
Silver – for creativity and protection
White – for peace, sincerity and devotion
Gold – for unity and prosperity

If you are marrying in church around a holiday the church may already be decorated. Ask your minister which decorations might be in place at the time of your ceremony.

Symbols can heighten the visual experience. You could choose to use an existing one such as a family crest. Alternatively, create your own emblem which captures your theme, represents your shared interests or makes a word play on your names.

For example a couple named Adam and Eve aptly chose an apple as their emblem. They embossed their Order of Service booklets with the apple symbol, tied an apple onto each pew end with ribbon, and dressed their bridesmaids in apple green. Their motif set the theme perfectly, appearing on their menus, place cards, bomboniere and wedding cake.

Flowers

The most traditional way of creating visual impact at a wedding ceremony is of course with flowers. See the Flowers chapter for advice on how to use flower arrangements to create a focal point, welcome guests and bring colour and vibrancy to your ceremony.

One Stop Tip

If you're getting married in church, ask your minister if they have a florist who usually arranges the flowers.

Customs and rituals

Including customs or rituals meaningful to you adds deeper significance to your ceremony. Some rituals are rooted in history, culture or religion whereas others are quite modern. Here are a few examples.

Scattered Petals

In an Old English tradition, flower girls would sprinkle petals before the bridal procession so the bride's path through life would always be happy and strewn with flowers. This is a lovely custom to incorporate in your ceremony if your venue allows it.

White dove release

The custom of releasing white doves on your wedding day dates back to medieval times. Doves build their nests together and mate for life so they have always symbolised love, peace and fidelity. It is said that if they are seen on your wedding day a happy home is assured.

Butterfly release

Less traditional but no less magical is the release of butterflies. They symbolise happiness, freedom and beauty, and releasing them can help restore their dwindling populations. Native Americans say if you whisper a wish to a butterfly, it will take it to the heavens and your wish shall be granted. The transformation of the butterfly also represents a new beginning, just as the bridal pair starts afresh as they are united in marriage.

Unity candle

During this ritual two candles, symbolising the bride and the groom as individuals, are brought together to light a single flame. This act symbolises the union of the two families and the couple's lifelong commitment to each other.

Hand fasting

The idea of 'tying the knot' originates from the old tradition of hand fasting. This is a pagan ritual which originally served as a kind of betrothal, and can be incorporated to honour Celtic heritage or Wiccan beliefs. The bride and groom link hands to form an infinity circle, and their wrists are loosely bound together with ribbon or cord to signify their union.

One Stop Tip

If another wedding is taking place before or after yours, you may be able to share the cost of your flowers with the other couple. Ask your officiant if this may be possible.

Sound

The words of many a beautiful ceremony have sadly been drowned out by the crashing waves on a beach or a room's poor acoustics. So when it comes to sound, the key thing is that your guests can actually hear your ceremony.

As a general rule, if you have over forty guests or are marrying outdoors you should use a microphone. Check your officiant has one they can bring along and ask a technically inclined friend to help set it up to ensure good sound quality – people love feeling useful!

A microphone for your readers will also come in handy. If you are having the ceremony filmed your videographer may choose to attach a microphone to your groom's lapel so your vows can be recorded.

Once you are sure you and your officiant will be clearly heard, background noise can add a great deal to the atmosphere. After all what could be more romantic than the sound of wind rustling through the trees or the exotic chirping of tropical birds?

Music

Once you have set the scene you can turn to what will probably be your greatest consideration when it comes to sound: music. Music can be used not only to create ambience but to connect you to some of the most emotionally charged moments in your life. Whether it's the song that was playing when you met or the one you first danced to, it has the ability to transport you back to that time and relive the emotions you felt at that moment. When you hear a song that was played on your wedding day, it will probably affect you in much the same way.

Go classical

Think about what kind of music would best fit your theme. If you are planning a traditional ceremony you might want the classical overtures of a string quartet. For a tranquil, romantic atmosphere the gentle strumming of a harpist might be appropriate.

Country music

Music can also be used to reflect your cultural heritage. Scottish brides might like the bagpipes played during their exit from the ceremony, whilst those of Scandinavian heritage could choose to be accompanied by a traditional accordion player.

Church harmonies

If you are marrying in church, why not ask the choir to learn harmonies for the hymns you have chosen? Don't forget to request that the church bells be rung at the end of the ceremony in celebration of your union.

Modern

Couples with more contemporary tastes may prefer a gospel choir, soloist or a band. Perhaps you have musical relatives or friends who can perform a solo or duet as their wedding gift to you.

Name that tune

Alternatively you may simply want to play some of your favourite pre-recorded music. Check your venue has a good sound system so your guests don't have to endure the tinny squealing of a cheap player.

Ceremony music checklist

- ☐ If you're marrying in church, find out if the church choir and organist are available that day. Are they familiar with the songs you have chosen?
- ☐ Check with your minister that your choice of music is acceptable.
- ☐ Make sure there's a good sound system if you want to play recorded music. If not, hire one yourself and make sure you test it well in advance.
- ☐ Make sure your musicians or choir have enough space to perform, and access to electrical plugs should they need it.
- ☐ Some hymns have more than one tune, so check your musicians know which one you want.

Hymns

Here are some examples for hymns and songs appropriate for wedding ceremonies:

All things bright and beautiful
Praise, my soul, the King of heaven
Morning has broken
Lord of all hopefulness
The Lord's my Shepherd
Amazing Grace
Amazing Grace (Wedding version)
Be our chief guest, Lord
Bind us together, Lord
Dear Lord and Father of Mankind
Give me joy in my heart
Guide me, o thou great Redeemer
Immortal, invisible

I vow to thee my country
Jerusalem
Lord of the dance
Love divine, all love excelling
Lead us heavenly father lead us
Jesus I have promised
Make me a channel of your peace

Music Ideas

Moment	Music Suggestions
Whilst guests wait for bride to arrive. Your choice should be joyful but unobtrusive – a harpist, string quartet, organ music, church or gospel choir.	*Classical:* Water Music – Handel Prelude, Air and Gavotte – Wesley The Prince of Denmark's March – Clarke *Modern:* Chapel of Love – The Dixie Cups Happy Together – The Turtles Wishin' and Hopin' (from the movie 'My Best Friend's Wedding') – Burt Bacharach Dream A Little Dream of Me – Gus Kahn
Entrance of the Bride. Choose something stately, dramatic or emotional.	*Classical:* Here Comes the Bride, Bridal Chorus from Lohengrin – Wagner The Arrival of the Queen of Sheba – Handel La Rejouissance – Handel I Was Glad – Parry *Modern:* God Only Knows – Beach Boys Shine on Shine on Me – Tony Backhouse Close to you – Burt Bacharach Unforgettable – Nat King Cole

Moment	Music Suggestions
The Signing of the Register. Choose something romantic or joyful.	**Classical:** Choral Prelude – Bach Canon in D – Pachelbel With piano or harp: Clair de Lune – Debussy With choir or soloist: Ave Maria – Schubert Amazing Grace – Newton **Modern:** Say a Little Prayer – Aretha Franklin Standing in the Water – Toni Nation Come Away With Me – Norah Jones I've got you under my skin – Cole Porter It Had To Be You – Harry Connick Jnr
The Recessional. Choose something uplifting and celebratory.	**Classical:** Wedding March from a Midsummer Night's Dream – Mendelssohn Music for the Royal Fireworks – Handel Triumphal March Opus 53 no 3 – Greig Grand March from Aida – Verdi Ode to Joy – Beethoven **Modern:** (Your love keeps lifting me) Higher and Higher - Jackie Wilson Signed, Sealed Delivered, I'm Yours – Stevie Wonder Oh Happy Day (from the movie 'Sister Act') – Edwin Hawkins

Scent

Does your ceremony location have its own unique scent? Perhaps it's the smell of wooden pews, the crisp freshness of mountain air, the fragrance of cut grass and roses in a garden or the humid, sultry scent of a rainforest.

Although not as obvious as that of sight or hearing, the scent of a place can still have strong emotional associations. Use it to add an unexpected extra dimension to your ceremony. Try overlaying the scent of your location with one of the following.

Herbs

You may like to include fragrant blooms in your flower arrangements. If so, consider mixing in a few herbs to balance the sweet floral fragrance. Try fresh mint leaves for an uplifting scent or basil for a fresh continental fragrance.

Incense

Known for its calming and healing properties, incense can be used to create a relaxed, enigmatic mood at your ceremony. Many associate sacred rituals with the scent of incense as it is burned in churches and temples. It's also a good choice if you're marrying outdoors as it's less likely to be blown out by a gust of wind than an oil burner. Choose from the huge variety of fragrances from the sweet, woody aroma of Sandalwood to the fresh, cinnamon-like notes of juniper.

Essential Oils

A potent alternative often used in spas, essential oils are also known as aromatherapy oils. Ask someone to light oil burners and place them around the room an hour before the ceremony begins so they have time to infuse the air. To create a serene, tranquil mood use an essential oil blend of geranium, mandarin and ylang ylang. Lemon myrtle, rosemary and grape-fruit can be combined for a fresh, vibrant scent or mix rose absolute and lavender oil for subtle romantic ambience.

> ### *SMUDGING*
>
> Many religious and spiritual traditions practise the burning of herbs for emotional and spiritual purification. You may want to incorporate the Native American tradition of 'smudging' to ritually cleanse your ceremony venue of negative influences.
> Ask a willing friend or relative to first set a positive intent, and then light a smudge stick (available from most health food and aromatherapy shops) well before your guests arrive. Allow it to smoulder whilst carrying it around the venue's perimeter. Direct the smoke into any corners, doors or windows where energy may stagnate. Extinguish the stick before guests arrive and enjoy the positive atmosphere.

Touch

Inspire your guests' sense of touch with embossed, velvet-covered or ribbon-tied Order of Service booklets, or the soft texture of rose petal confetti. Here are some other ways to make your ceremony more sensual.

Comfort

Are the seats too hard? Is there enough seating for everyone? If not you may find many guests, arriving early and then standing throughout the ceremony, become quite tired. Ladies will be in their best high heels and standing in these for close to an hour can become uncomfortable.

Temperature

If you're marrying in winter check your venue's heating will be turned on, and if you are marrying outside on a summer's day advise out of town guests on comfortable dress. In hot weather there should be plenty of shade. Consider distributing paper fans for guests to cool themselves with and check the venue has sufficient ventilation and air conditioning. Your guests are sure to appreciate a water station.

Taste

Enjoying the day through the sense of taste is usually something reserved for the mouth watering delights of the reception dinner. Depending on the location however you may wish to serve canapés and soft drinks to those waiting for the ceremony to begin.

Writing Your Own Vows

Writing your own vows can be a poignant way of personalising the central part of your marriage ceremony. But composing the most magical promise of love you have ever created takes time, and some serious soul searching. Before embarking on this journey be sure your groom is as keen on the idea as you are, and that your officiant does not object.

Something old, something new

Start by looking for inspiration from traditional marriage vows that have stood the test of time. These contain moving and trusted words that have joined couples together for generations, eloquently expressing the key promises upon which a happy marriage can be founded.

You may choose to combine phrases from traditional wedding vows with your own words. A favourite is the traditional Protestant query,

Will you love her/him, comfort her/him, honour and keep her/him… as long as you both shall live?

which many couples choose to incorporate into their own wedding vows.

Make it personal

Be sure to express what's unique about the two of you. Ask yourselves, what does marriage mean to you? If you are from different backgrounds, you could promise to support and uphold both heritages whilst together building traditions of your own. If marrying for you is about having a family together, you may want to include a something like

I take you, (Name), to be the father / mother of my children, to have and to hold...

I promise...

A vow is really a promise, so focus on meaningful promises and commitments that you would like to make to each other. Your words should be heartfelt and sincere, but avoid long descriptions on the nature of your love for one another which are better kept for the speeches. You could for example pledge to:

- Love, honour, respect and cherish each other
- Be kind, trusting and tolerant
- Support each other in times of trouble
- Encourage one another
- Respect each other's individuality
- Be understanding and patient towards each other
- Stay together for life
- Be faithful and honest
- Be a good friend
- Bring fun and laughter into the marriage

Remember that your vows should be written as a public declaration of your commitment to each other, so avoid any overly intimate details. You should keep them short, preferably under two minutes. It's advisable to discuss them with your officiant, who with all their experience may have lots of helpful suggestions.

Sample vows

I promise to love, comfort and encourage you, to be open and honest with you, and stay with you forsaking all others as long as we both shall live.

I promise to love, respect and honour you, sharing your plans, dreams and emotions, through all the trials and tribulations of life, as well as the joyous times, caring for you in lifelong commitment.

I promise to be your confidante, always ready to share your hopes, dreams and plans for the future.

Practice makes perfect

A sentence that looks great when written can be difficult to understand or overlong when spoken. For this reason it's a good idea to practise your vows out loud. Check there's nothing that might trip up your tongue and make adjustments until it sounds right. Read slowly and clearly, and practise projecting your voice so your guests will be able to hear you.

Whether you want to recite your vows independently or repeat them, make sure you give your officiant a copy. That way if your nerves kick in and your mind goes blank, you can just repeat them after your officiant.

Ceremony Seating

Traditionally friends and family of the bride sit on the left side of the aisle and friends and family of the groom sit on the right. If there are more guests from one family than another, groomsmen should even out the seating.

Parents, grandparents, and siblings usually sit in the first row. If the bride or groom's parents are divorced but both will be attending, the mother (and her husband) can sit in the first row and the father (and his wife) in the second. It is also fine to separate them by a few rows to avoid any tension. All other family members sit behind immediate family.

To avoid any confusion or misunderstandings, you may want to prepare cards bearing each guest's name for the front two rows. Groomsmen should be on hand up to an hour before the start of the ceremony to escort guests to their seats, offering their right arm to female guests.

The groom's mother is usually seated takes her seat by the aisle about fifteen minutes before the ceremony begins, and the mother of the bride should be escorted by a groomsman to her seat on the opposite side of the aisle just before the processional.

Don't forget the parents!

Always remember that although this is your wedding, it's also a profoundly significant moment for your parents. Make them feel extra special by arranging for a letter from you to be waiting for them on your mother's seat just prior to the start of the ceremony. In it you could thank your parents for all they have done for you, or perhaps express the hope that your marriage will be as fulfilling as theirs. They are bound to feel touched to be honoured in such a thoughtful way.

Cost Saving Tips for your Ceremony

- Hold your ceremony and reception in the same place so you are charged only one fee for the location.
- Get married in a beautiful spot which does not need decorating like a rose garden or beach.
- Plan floral decorations which can be moved to your reception venue.
- Get a musical friend to sing or play a meaningful song as their wedding gift to you.

What Happens When?

Whereas civil ceremonies offer great flexibility, religious ones usually follow a similar sequence of events. Ask your minister to review this with you so you know exactly what will happen when as each service will differ slightly.

The greeting/call to worship

Your minister introduces the service and welcomes your guests.

The charge to the couple

At this point the bride and groom confirm they have come together of their own free will. The Protestant ceremony for example asks, "Will you have this man/woman to be your wedded (husband/wife) to live together in holy matrimony...?"

The giving away

When the minister asks "Who gives this woman to be married to this man?" the bride's father replies, "I do."

The vows

This is the moment when you promise to love, trust, and honor each other, "to have and to hold ... for better or for worse." Modern couples often choose to substitute the word "cherish" in place of the bride's traditional pledge to "obey".

The exchange of rings

The bride and groom place a wedding ring on each other's left ring finger and say, "With this ring, I thee wed."

The pronouncement

The minister now declares that you are legally married. The traditional words are "I now pronounce you man and wife. Those whom God has joined together, let no man put asunder." The officiant then tells the groom he may kiss the bride.

One Stop Review

- ☐ Choose a celebrant you trust with good public speaking skills.
- ☐ Find a stunning, unique venue by seeking out unusual locations.
- ☐ Use all five senses to create a special ambience.
- ☐ Add deeper significance to your ceremony with meaningful rituals.
- ☐ Create emotionally charged moments with well chosen music.
- ☐ Consider personalising your ceremony by writing your own vows.

Notes

_____

_____

_____

_____

_____

_____

_____

_____

_____

_____

_____

_____

_____

_____

_____

_____

_____

_____

_____

_____

_____

_____

_____

_____

_____

_____

Notes

_____

_____

_____

_____

_____

_____

_____

_____

_____

_____

_____

_____

_____

_____

_____

_____

_____

_____

_____

_____

_____

_____

_____

_____

_____

_____

The Reception

The tradition of the wedding reception dates back to a time when the whole village would gather together to enjoy a sumptuous feast in the town square. Today it continues as a celebration of the destiny that brought the bridal couple together, and a chance to thank friends and family for their love and support by throwing a party to remember.

This chapter will show you how to organise that party with maximum style and minimum stress. It will guide you through each stage, from the dreaded seating plans and the more enjoyable wine tasting, to choosing your table decorations and the evening's entertainment. You will get tips and tricks on how to choose your venue and create a magical, memorable atmosphere. But most importantly you will see how to make yourself and your guests feel as special as possible – without blowing the budget.

Choosing the Venue

Picture yourself at a beachside restaurant, celebrating late into a balmy night with all your friends and family as the ocean waves lap the shore. Or perhaps you'd enjoy a more intimate gathering at a hinterland hideaway overlooking picturesque mountains veiled in mist? With the huge array of reception venues available to the modern bride, whatever your wish it can surely be granted.

Get the look

Shortlist anywhere with unique décor like a spiral staircase, roaring open fireplace, wood panelled walls or sparkling chandelier. These will be appreciated by your guests and provide wonderful photo opportunities.

Is there a place of natural beauty near your ceremony venue like a grand old house or art gallery? Look in magazines, search the internet and check the Yellow Pages to find venues with that special ingredient.

Also short-list venues which combine several picturesque locations. You could for example hold your ceremony in a winery's lakeside chapel and your welcome drinks on the veranda overlooking the vines, followed by a lavish dinner in the main building's opulent ballroom.

Cost Saving Tips for your Venue

- To save on furniture, crockery and linen hire, choose a venue such as a hotel which already has everything you need.
- Restaurants which usually close at weekends may offer discounts for Saturday wedding hire, so ask around.
- Pool the whole family's fairy lights to decorate the venue. String them from the ceiling and around railings.
- If your favours are attractive, pile them in the middle of the table for great centrepieces that save on the cost of flowers.
- Create a romantic atmosphere on a budget by illuminating the room with plenty of candlelight.

Compare venues

Once you have short-listed your favourite venues, start phoning round and ask how many people each can accommodate. A venue catering for slightly more than your expected number of guests will create a warm, sociable ambience without seeming overcrowded. Ask for an idea of the price per head for food and drink as well as the cost of hiring the venue. Also request a full price list of optional extras such as hire of a cake knife, table decorations or chair covers.

Soon you will have narrowed your search down to a few places that you will want to visit personally. Check the outlook from the windows and consider whether the room's furnishings will coordinate with your colour scheme. Meet with the staff who will be serving your guests to get a feel for their attitude and quality of service. If the venue provides catering, try the food and ask to see sample menus and pricings.

Reception Venue Questions

- ☐ Will the venue comfortably accommodate everyone?
- ☐ How far is it from your ceremony location?
- ☐ Is there enough space to greet guests?
- ☐ Are there enough toilets?
- ☐ Is there sufficient parking?
- ☐ Are there facilities for disabled or elderly guests?
- ☐ Is there a secure cloakroom where coats and handbags can be hung?
- ☐ What is the venue's position on licensing laws?
- ☐ Do they provide catering?
- ☐ If so can you see sample menus and pricings?
- ☐ Is there adequate linen, seating, glassware, crockery and cutlery?
- ☐ Can guests with special dietary needs be catered for?

- ☐ What table decorations does the venue already have?
- ☐ Are any other decorations included such as fairy lights or chair covers?
- ☐ Is a sound system and microphone available for use?
- ☐ Is there enough room to dance?
- ☐ Are there noise restrictions?
- ☐ Is there room for a band or DJ?
- ☐ Is there nearby overnight accommodation?

THE RECEIVING LINE

A receiving line gives you, your groom and both sets of parents a great opportunity to greet each guest personally and thank them for coming. Some couples like to do this as guests exit the ceremony but most prefer to welcome them as they arrive at the reception. In the conventional receiving line the mother and father of the bride receive guests first, followed by the groom's parents and then the happy couple themselves. There is, however, no reason why you should stick with the traditional arrangement. If you are having an informal wedding you may even choose to do without a receiving line at all.

Creating Ambience

Whether you are hosting a civilized luxurious affair or throwing a wild party, to create the right ambience you need a multi-sensory experience.

Start by imagining the place you feel most comfortable and happy together. How does it look, sound, smell, taste and feel? Focus on recreating that special atmosphere by appealing to every one of the senses.

Sight

So you've chosen the perfect reception venue – but how do you create that wow factor when your guests first walk into the room?

To begin with, consider how you can highlight the room's best features. Perhaps there is a window which perfectly frames the sunset or French windows which can be opened to catch breezes and take in more of the view. You may want to rearrange existing furniture to create a more intimate feel.

Lighting

For a relaxed ambience, light levels should be subtle and unobtrusive. Steer clear of harsh central ceiling lights which cast a bland, even glow over everything. Focus instead on creating intimate pools of light and shade. Check sunset times to plan when you want the lights dimmed up and the candles lit.

You may want to use venue decorators or lighting hire specialists to help you create the feel you want. Up lighters and down lights can transform a room by illuminating architectural features, cosy corners, plants or works of art. Outside you may want to illuminate pathways with flares or hurricane lamps. String fairy lights or glowing lanterns through trees to add a touch of magic.

Venue Decorations

If you are working with a venue that possesses a beauty and enigma of its own, it will probably not need much embellishment. A stunning room is best offset by the simplest decorations such as flowers and candlelight. Create the right ambience by dressing your space stylishly with elements that carry through your theme, using decoration to highlight and complement the unique features of the room rather than over-powering them.

To make your guests feel extra welcome you can frame the entrance to your reception with topiary trees. Achieve a relaxed lounge feel by placing hired potted plants around the room. Chair covers can give the event a sense of occasion, and you might even choose to decorate ceilings and walls with swathes of translucent fabric in your theme colour. See the 'Wedding Flowers' chapter for ideas on decorative floral displays.

Laying the Table

From crisp white linen to beaded silks, your tables can be decorated in any imaginable colour and texture. Wedding hire companies can prepare a whole place setting for you with coor-dinating china, cutlery, napkins, table runners, glassware and chair coverings. This is a great way to get an idea of how your tables will look before the big day.

If you are using the venue's existing linen, crockery and cutlery there are still endless ways to create the look you want. Traditional thick white linen tablecloths have a classic elegance of their own, but if you want to dress them up you can hire translucent organza overlays in your theme colour. Otherwise just add spectacular table centrepieces in your wedding colour and tie matching delicate organza bows around napkins.

Classic table decorations

Some kind of central decoration is a must for reception tables. The best ones are enchanting displays which can be admired and enjoyed without obstructing peoples' view of each other. They should either be low enough for your guests to talk over, or high enough to allow them to see each other under-neath.

The romantic rays of **candlelight** have long been used to create a cosy atmosphere of warmth and intimacy. Tea lights in frosted glass holders are particularly attractive as their diffused, flickering glow lights up a space without the glare of a bare flame.

Candelabras are an enduring favourite, or you might prefer the more contemporary look of a collection of pillar candles in different heights. Simply sprinkle fresh rose petals around the base and place the whole arrangement on a framed mirror. The candle light will be reflected up, illuminating the whole table in a soft ethereal glow.

Flowers are of course the classic centrepiece decoration. See the 'Wedding Flowers' chapter for ideas.

Themed table decorations

Expressing your theme through your table centrepieces is a great way to tie the separate elements of your day together and bring a sense of fun and individuality to the festivities. Here are some ideas.

Waterfront

For a striking arrangement, submerge bright gerberas or lilies in water filled glass spaghetti vases. Alternatively, fill large glass bowls with water, river pebbles, swirls of greenery, coral, shells and one or two goldfish. Use lobster or starfish shaped lollipops for bomboniere, each tied to a place card with a sea-blue ribbon.

Tropical

Display a collection of exotic star fruit, kiwis, papayas and pineapples adorned with a sprinkling of frangipani blooms.

For favours, use wicker fans each garnished with a single orchid.

Autumn

Fruit place card holders are ideal for an autumn wedding. Make an incision into an apple or pear and use it to hold a place card. If your colour scheme includes gold or silver, spray paint your fruit to match. Alternatively, write your guests' names with a gold marker on brightly coloured fallen leaves. Spray them with laminate to make them rigid and glossy.

Christmas

Place an iced gingerbread house in the centre of each table or fill glass vases with twinkling fairy lights, tinsel and baubles. On a tight budget? Just wrap your bomboniere in Christmas paper, tie them with ribbon and stack them in the middle of the table.

Asian

Decorate tables with bamboo table runners, scattered Singapore orchids and colourful glowing Chinese lanterns. Continue your theme with fortune cookie bomboniere or fill mini Chinese take-out cartons with sweets and tie with crimson ribbon.

Colour

Carry your colour theme throughout with matching napkin rings, table overlays or floral arrangements. Colourful fruit sculptures make delightful centrepieces. You may even find that a bowl of pears, lemons or limes matches the exact hue of your bridesmaids' dresses.

Edible

Fill baskets with an assortment of mouth-watering breads like rye bread, pumpernickel, sun dried tomato bread and grissini. The variation in texture will be beautifully enhanced by soft candle light and your guests will enjoy digging in to it. As an accompaniment you could ask your caterer to provide a selection of delicious spreads such as garlic butter, olive oil and balsamic vinegar.

For creative ideas on table numbers, place cards and favours, see the Stationery chapter.

Sound

If sight sets the scene, it is sound that sets the mood. They both blend with the other senses to create a seamless multi-layered experience often referred to as a 'great atmosphere' where each element becomes hard to define.

Your most important consideration when it comes to sound should be that the speeches can be well heard. Music and other background sound should only be used as a backdrop to these, so discuss sound levels carefully with your musicians.

Also be sure to check there is a microphone on site for your speakers to use. Chances are they will be nervous and less able to project their voices than they are when practising. The acoustics of the room will also be dampened by the number of people and the amount of furniture. As a general rule, if you have forty guests or more you should use a microphone. Your venue may have one available for such occasions but if not you can always hire one. Ask a technically inclined friend to set up the microphone well in advance and test it for sound quality and volume.

Live music

The melody which welcomes your guests to the reception will set the tone for the rest of the evening. For a refined, sophisticated feel you could opt for a **string quartet** (two violins, a viola and a cello). Such ensembles can perform a selection of popular classics and modern music sure to please your guests.

A **jazz trio**, consisting of a saxophone, guitar and bass player, can create a classy, upbeat atmosphere with a selection of Swing and Latin tunes.

Solo musicians can be just as effective and are usually less expensive. A guitarist will create a relaxed ambience with jazz, classical or flamenco music. And if it's romance you're after, there's nothing quite like the enchanting strumming of a **harpist**.

For suggestions on music for the after dinner dancing, see the After Dinner Entertainment section at the end of this chapter.

Pre-recorded music

You may prefer to set the mood with some of your favourite pre-recorded music. Check your venue has a good sound system – if not you should borrow or hire one. It will also give you peace of mind to know that the sound volume and quality has been checked by your venue's staff or a trusted friend.

Your choice of music should reflect your theme and personal tastes. Songs with a lively vibe or ones with a more relaxed feel may be appropriate depending on the mood you want to create. Music that works well includes easy listening, jazz, pop or chill out albums. Flamenco will create a lively continental feel, or for a touch of mysticism try some Indian classical music or New Age birdsong. Just avoid anything too solemn – and check that the lyrics speak of love and joy rather than heartache and rejection!

Making an Entrance

One of your proudest moments will undoubtedly be when you first enter the dining room to be introduced by your MC as the new Mr and Mrs. Many couples like their entrance to be accompanied by some upbeat, celebratory music. This is played during the walk to your seat, from the moment you are announced to when you take your place at the top table.

You may also want music played during the cutting of the cake or the throwing of the garter. Your first dance as husband and wife will be the most important song of all, and you can read more about this later in this chapter.

IDEAS FOR ENTRANCE MUSIC

Canon In D – Pachelbel
Perfect Day – Hoku
Escape – Enrique Inglasias
Celebration – Kool and the Gang
Beautiful Day – U2
Hallellujah chorus – Handel's 'Messiah'
Heaven is a Place on Earth – Belinda Carlisle
You and Me Song – Wannadies

Scent

The scent of your venue will provide the backdrop against which the events of the day unfold. Whether this is the cosy scent of a pine panelled interior or the fragrance of freshly cut grass, it is sure to create a unique ambience.

Aromatherapy oil diffusers or scented candles can be used throughout your welcome drinks reception. Select fragrances similar to those in your floral arrangements so that strong scents complement rather than clash with one another.

At your reception meal, the fragrance from any floral centrepieces should be kept subtle to avoid overpowering the taste and aroma of the food. Aromatherapy oil and candles scented with floral notes are not usually appropriate since the sweet scent can clash with the savoury aroma of food, an effect which can be somewhat sickly. Instead, choose herbal candles fragranced with basil or rosemary which will better compliment your food.

A special touch which will be much appreciated by your guests is a fragrant vase or basket of flowers placed in the bathrooms and dressing area. A bottle of perfume and some hand moisturiser is also a thoughtful gesture.

Touch

The comfort of the seats and the amount of personal space available are key elements to ensure your guests' wellbeing. Heating, open fireplaces or air conditioning can be used to create a pleasant room temperature.

For outdoor receptions, ensure there is adequate shade and a back-up plan in case of rain. Braziers can be used to keep people warm well into the night, and marquees can be hired with integrated air conditioning systems.

Taste

What better way to celebrate your marriage than a delicious feast and festive toast with friends and family? Whether it's wine, canapés, a sit-down meal or informal buffet, you will want to stimulate those taste buds with a fusion of tantalising flavours. Hunt out experienced caterers who combine excellent food with quality fast service. Food and drink is usually the largest single expense of a wedding so ensure you get your money's worth.

Pop the cork!

The perfect way to kick off the celebrations is with welcome drinks. This is usually the point at which photographs of the bride and groom are taken. If you want to enjoy this chance to mingle with your guests, your welcome drinks may have to extend for two hours or longer. However with a beautiful view, adequate seating and plenty of drinks and canapés, the time is sure to fly by.

When it comes to what drinks to serve it must be said that champagne truly never goes out of style. But if you prefer something more unusual, try serving a signature drink invented by you and your groom and named in your honour. A variation on something with a bright colour works well – try a champagne cocktail, pina colada or fruit punch. Alternatively, serve a drink named after your honeymoon destination like a Blue Hawaiian.

Food

Planning a successful menu is all about choosing dishes which will tickle all tastebuds. If you are inviting lots of children or elderly relatives, spicy dishes are probably out. Ask guests to inform you of any special dietary requirements well in advance. This information will be useful for the meeting with your caterer when you can discuss requirements in greater detail and view sample menus.

A **sit-down silver service** dinner usually includes three

courses, coffee and wedding cake. This is the most formal and traditional but also usually the most expensive option, since you will have to pay for a larger number of waiting staff.

Slightly less formal, a **fork buffet** allows your guests to choose from an assortment of hot and cold food so they can decide for themselves what they want to eat. Table settings are still set formally with decorative centrepieces, and a seating plan is usually used.

As the name suggests, a **finger buffet** does not require cutlery. Guests usually mingle freely, although you may choose to seat them. This is a less expensive option, but if it's a long day people may get tired of standing.

For style on a budget consider a **cocktail reception**, usually held between 5.00 and 7.00 pm. Be sure your guests know to expect canapés rather than a five-course meal by wording your invitations with something like "Please join us for cocktails and hors d'oeuvres following the ceremony." When choosing your canapés, watch your costs or your bill could end up rivalling that of a formal seated dinner. It's also worth bearing in mind that guests are likely to consume more alcohol than if they are seated.

For an elegant celebration on any budget, why not host **afternoon tea**? Whether held in a simple church hall or a grand stately home this can be an original way to celebrate. Afternoon tea is usually held between 2.00 and 5.00 pm and the menu can include a delicious selection of cheeses, sandwiches, scones, fruit, brownies, cookies, and of course an assortment of fine teas.

You might choose to combine several ideas, perhaps having a soup served in a formal sit-down style starter with a buffet for the main course. Whatever you choose to do, make sure it's your kind of party.

Wedding Wine

Some venues which specialise in weddings offer a complimentary wine tasting session – and who could refuse? A good wine connoisseur will recommend quality wines in any price range, so be specific about your budget and taste, taste, taste!

If you are not given this option you can still choose the wine yourselves. Buy a few bottles in your price range, invite some friends round and get tasting. Steer clear of less popular wine styles such as heavily oaked chardonnays or anything too sweet or acidic.

> ## One Stop Tip
>
> Buying your own wine? Then expect a discount. Wines sold in shops include a fee for handling and display, so ask for a 10 to 15 percent off the price if buying in bulk.

Alcohol consumption is usually highest at the start of the event during the welcome drinks. It tends to tail off during the meal and then pick up again during the after dinner dancing. With this in mind you can ask your venue staff if wedding guests usually drink enough to merit an all-you-can-drink package.

Unless your guests are heavy drinkers, it's often cheaper to pay by the bottle than to be charged by the hour. Just make sure you ask staff to inform you or a relative when and if your limit is reached. If it's nearing the end of the night, you might decide to pay for the extra few bottles anyway.

Cost Saving Tips for Food and Drink

- You can radically cut costs if you find a BYO (bring your own) reception venue and buy wine and beer in bulk.

Just check to see what corkage fees your venue charges.

- Serve only wine and beer and let people pay for their own spirits.
- Serving a fruit punch as a welcome drink is a cheaper option than sparkling wine.
- Establish a limit on the bar tab and let guests pay for their drinks after this is reached.
- If you want to foot the whole alcohol bill but are concerned about escalating costs, consider a lunchtime reception as people generally drink less during the day.
- Stop the free bar during the meal and instead station a few bottles of red and white wine on each table.
- Serve tapas-style platters of cold food for the starter, and team it with a hot dish for the main course.
- Choose a creative chef who dresses up cheap ingredients with sauces, fruit or stuffing to make them seem really special.
- Guests are often too full to manage pudding and wedding cake, so spend your money on a really delicious cake and serve large helpings with ice cream as desert.
- A stylish and cheaper alternative to the traditional sit-down meal is a gourmet picnic – the perfect accompaniment to a garden wedding.

Wedding Cake

As tradition says, when you cut your wedding cake you are cutting your first slice of married life. As the first act you perform together as husband and wife, this represents the plunge you take as you embark on a new life together.

Wedding cakes date back to Roman times when a thin wheat cake, representing bounty, was broken over the bride's head to ensure fertility. Thankfully over the centuries this tradition has evolved into the custom of eating the wedding cake which we all know and love!

Your cake is a symbol of your celebration, and sharing it with friends and family represents the sharing of your happiness and good fortune. Consequently the most important thing is that it is delicious – a cake which looks great but tastes average will not go down well. To check it's as tasty as it looks, sample different cakes from your cake maker when you meet to discuss requirements.

Wedding cakes are made up of several tiers, either separated by pillars or stacked on top of each other in the 'American' style. Often the top layer is kept to be eaten on the couple's first year anniversary or the birth of their first child.

What's your Flavour?

The classic wedding cake is the three tiered fruit cake decorated with thick icing and sugar flowers, but for something more contemporary try one of the following:

- Carrot cake
- Chocolate mud cake
- Caramel mud cake
- Vanilla sponge cake
- Tia Maria mud cake
- Orange and poppy cake
- Banana cake
- Butter cake

Cake Decoration

The white wedding cake is a popular classic, but there are plenty of other stylish options open to you. A cake smothered in white Belgian chocolate decorated with pink roses is an elegant twist on tradition. Whatever you choose, your cake should compliment your theme and colour scheme.

Fresh or sugar flowers are usually used as decoration. Sugar flowers can look incredibly lifelike and, unlike fresh flowers, they won't wilt. On the other hand a simple posy of fresh flowers for the top of the cake looks stunning, and will usually be cheaper than sugar flowers. If you want to use fresh flowers make sure your florist and cake maker are in close communication.

Shop around to find a good cake maker who is skilled at making the type of cake your want. If you want intricate sugar craft, choose someone who specialises in this technique, whereas if it's a croquembouche you're after it's better to go with someone skilled in chocolate and patisserie.

Themed Cake Ideas

Romantic

Ask your cake maker to drape your cake in swathes of icing and embellish it with sugar flowers, ribbons, greenery or fresh flowers matching your bridal bouquet.

Croquembouche

This traditional French wedding cake consists of individual puffs of choux pastry filled with a vanilla crème patisserie, all held together with a delicious cobweb of caramel.

Themed

Seek out a talented novelty cake maker who can create a masterpiece which matches your theme. For example the cake for a seaside wedding cake might incorporate starfish, shells, fish or seahorses.

Miniatures

For something unusual, stack tiny iced cakes or a variety of small puddings so your guests can pick their favourite dessert.

Cappuccino

Want to have your cake and eat it? With a Cappuccino cake you can, with three different layers of cake in each tier. The bottom layer consists of chocolate mud cake, the middle of coffee cake and the top of white chocolate cake.

> ## One Stop Tip
> The size of your wedding cake will depend on the number of guests you have invited and whether you want to keep the top tier. Allow at least one slice per guest, more if you are serving it as dessert.

Meeting your (cake) maker

Do not feel that you have to go along to your cake maker with specific ideas of how you want your cake to look. A true professional will be able to recommend designs and ideas to fit the theme, budget and feel of your wedding. To help them out, you will need to take along as much visual information on your wedding day as possible. This could include a swatch of fabric from your dress and that of your bridesmaids, photographs of the reception venue and a folder of ideas gathered from magazines or the Internet.

Your cake maker will need to know approximately how many people the cake needs to feed, whether you will be keeping the top tier, and if the cake will be taken home by guests or eaten as dessert. Explain the feel, theme and colour scheme of your wedding and see what they suggest. Ask to see photographs of their past creations and any magazines on hand for inspiration. Ask if the cake will be baked fresh or if it will be frozen, and insist on tasting a slice before you place your order.

One Stop Tip

If your cake will be doubling as dessert, ask your caterers to serve it with a delicious accompaniment like raspberry coulis, vanilla ice cream or chocolate sauce.

Transporting your cake

Ask for detailed instructions on how your cake should be transported to your reception venue and how it is to be stored. Some cakes should be kept in an air conditioned room as refrigeration causes the colours to run. Be sure to inform your reception venue of any storage requirements well in advance.

You will also need to check that your venue has a cake stand and cake knife. If they do not, ask your cake maker if they know where you would be able to hire these from.

Cutting the Cake

The cake is usually cut after the speeches, but if you want it to double as dessert you might like to cut it before the main meal is served to allow time for it to be divided into portions and served as pudding. When the time comes the bride holds the knife in her right hand and the groom overlaps his on top, and together they cut the bottom layer. Afterwards you may want to link arms and sip champagne. Following with a kiss is always a crowd pleaser.

Cost Saving Tips for your cake

- Save on delivery costs by asking a trusted friend or relative to collect the cake and transport it to the reception.
- A simple, tasty, elegant cake will cost less than one with lots of time-consuming decoration.
- The more cake there is to decorate, the more it will cost. So for a wedding party of 170 people, order an ornamented cake large enough to serve 100 and a plainly iced 'kitchen cake' to serve the rest. No one need ever know!
- Choosing a design from the cake maker's style book is usually cheaper than having one specially designed for you.
- By all means try to cut costs, but never compromise on flavour – it's better to order a delicious but simple cake than a pretty but tasteless one. Go to cake tastings to check you are happy with what you order and beware of companies charging really low prices.

Seating Plan

The task of organising seating plans has the reputation of being a bride's worst headache. However with a little forethought and some common sense it can be surprisingly straightforward.

Organising a wedding is in some ways similar to planning any sort of celebration, so think back to the last party you organised. What did you do if you knew one of your friends would not know anyone else there? Perhaps you arranged for them to get a lift to the party with another guest or sat them next to some of your more sociable friends. Use techniques that have worked well before to put guests at ease and you will lay the groundwork for a relaxed, enjoyable meal. The golden rule is to make your guests comfortable, and how you go about this is up to you.

The time to start planning your seating is when you have a final headcount and a floor plan of how the tables will be arranged. Seating plans originate from the idea of intermingling your two families so they can get to know each other. Whilst this is great in theory, it's also fine to seat members of the same family together.

To seat or not to seat?

Whilst it is important to reserve the top table for the bridal party, if you are having a relatively small wedding you could choose free seating for other guests. This arrangement works well if everyone already knows each other.

Alternatively, tell your guests which table to sit on but leave it to them to choose where to sit within that table. If you still want to allocate seating for the bridal party, print out place cards only for the top table.

It's important to have a seating plan for larger weddings as this enables guests to be seated quickly. It also allows you to seat people who know few other guests with a friendly, welcoming group and makes it easy to separate people who do not get along. Refer to the Stationery chapter for advice on how to put together a seating plan.

Seating Checklist

- ☐ To plan your seating draw the tables on a large piece of card and write each guest's name on a post-it note so you can move them around until you're happy.
- ☐ Always seat couples together.
- ☐ Reserve seats nearest the top table for your closest family and friends to mark them out as special.

- ☐ Seat guests who do not know anyone else with a friendly, welcoming crowd.
- ☐ Put groups of friends together rather than breaking them up.
- ☐ Seat singles on the same table.
- ☐ So far as possible, avoid seating someone on a table of people who they have never met before. Instead, seat them with some people they know and some they don't.
- ☐ Seat divorced couples or guests who do not get on as far away from each other as possible.

Table layouts

Some brides like the idea of a horseshoe configuration, others prefer long rectangular tables. Round tables are great for conversation and they avoid any hierarchy which might cause friction.

The 'open' round table is another popular option, particularly for top table arrangements. Here guests are seated around only part of the table, with an open section so they can still be seen by other guests. Discuss your table layout options well in advance with your caterer or venue staff.

Seating the Top Table

There is of course a traditional way to seat the top table, but for many reasons modern couples often choose to do it their own way. Sometimes this is because one or both sets of parents are divorced or deceased, or even because the bridal party is simply too large to seat at one table.

The most important thing is not that the 'rules' are followed but that everyone has a great time. So if you think your chief bridesmaid would enjoy catching up with her old school friends, why not seat her with them instead of with you?

The traditional top table sees the bride and groom in the centre with the wedding party seated either side of them, like this:

Chief Brides-maid	Father of the Groom	Mother of the Bride	Groom	Bride	Father of the Bride	Mother of the Groom	Best Man

If both sets of parents prefer to sit with their spouses, consider this alternative:

Chief Brides-maid	Father of the Bride	Mother of the Bride	Groom	Bride	Father of the Groom	Mother of the Groom	Best Man

In instances where one or both sets of parents are divorced you may need to get creative. If there is the remotest chance of friction, speak with all parties concerned separately and get their input. Here are some options.

If the bride's parents have remarried:

Bride's Step-father	Chief Brides-maid	Father of the Groom	Mother of the Bride	Groom	Bride	Father of the Bride	Mother of the Groom	Best Man	Bride's Step-mother

If the groom's parents have remarried:

Groom's Step-father	Chief Brides-maid	Father of the Groom	Mother of the Bride	Groom	Bride	Father of the Bride	Mother of the Groom	Best Man	Groom's Step-mother

or:

Best Man	Groom's Step-mother	Groom's Father	Mother of the Bride	Groom	Bride	Father of the Bride	Mother of the Groom	Groom's Step-father	Chief Brides-maid

If both the bride & groom's parents have remarried:

Groom's Step mother	Bride's Step father	Chief Brides- maid	Father of the Groom	Mother of the Bride	Groom	Bride	Father of the Bride	Mother of the Groom	Best Man	Bride's Step mother	Groom's Step father

Another solution is simply to seat the bridal party on the top table with their partners, and let each parent and their spouse host a table of their own.

After Dinner Entertainment

Your choice of entertainment is very much a matter of personal choice. However you should consider the age range of your guests and what kind of music they usually enjoy dancing to.

Choose music with as wide an appeal as possible – something that will make people hit the dance floor at the earliest opportunity. Seventies disco or Swing tunes work well as they are popular across the generations. For a fairly young crowd you could choose 80s classics or modern pop.

One Stop Tip

It is standard practice to supply a simple meal for your musicians, photographer and videographer during the course of the evening.

You can either dance between courses, or let your guests enjoy their meals before the dancing begins. Just be sure to communicate the sequence of events to your band or DJ. It's also wise to ask for a signed contract which details any special requests you may have of your musicians (see Get It In Writing later in this chapter).

DJ or Band?

BAND	
Pros	**Cons**
Salsa, Swing, Country or Jazz – whatever your preference, you can easily find a band out there with a passion for playing it	Usually costs more than a DJ
	Songs never sound quite the same as the original recording
Gives the party more atmosphere and a greater sense of occasion	Coordinating a group of people to perform can be difficult
This could be the only time in your life when you will go to the effort and expense of hiring a band	Your venue may have sound level restrictions which prohibit a band from performing

DJ	
Pros	**Cons**
Songs sound as they did when recorded, with no surprises or bad covers	If your DJ uses a pre-recorded play list, they will not be able to choose whichever song best fits the mood
Usually costs less than a band	
Lights and other props are often included in the price	If you don't carefully edit the song list, be warned – you may fall prey to your DJ's standard wedding repertoire
DJs have a larger music selection to choose from	

> ## One Stop Tip
> DJ or band – or why not hire both? Many brides now hire a band/DJ combo so the DJ can spin discs while the band takes a break.

Hiring Musicians

Once you've decided on a musical genre, you will need to find musicians to perform it. Start by speaking to any musical friends you may have. They will know who's who on the music scene and may be able to direct you to some of the best talent around. Perhaps they know of an up and coming DJ or local band who are just the thing you need.

There are plenty of great undiscovered musicians performing in clubs and bars, so keep your eye out and ask around. Usually they will charge much less than a 'wedding' band.

Bridal fairs are a great place to meet musicians, and you may even be able to see them perform whilst you are there. You can also contact wedding bands and DJs listed in the Yellow Pages or speak to wedding music agents.

Try Before You Buy

If you are hiring a band be sure to listen to them before you hire them, as their live performance may be quite different from their demo tape. Go along to their next gig and ask them to perform any favourite songs you want included. If they do not know the song, are they happy to learn it for your wedding?

Make Special Requests

The best way to be sure the music will be to your liking is

to request a copy of the band or DJ's song list. Underline songs you want them to perform and cross out those you dislike. This will give them an idea of your taste so they can choose similar songs to perform for the rest of the night.

Get it in Writing

Insist all the important points are listed in a written contract. This should include:

☐ The full names of each musician who will perform
☐ What they will wear
☐ Time of arrival, set up and departure
☐ Number and duration of sets
☐ Space and electrical requirements
☐ Special requirements, such as any new songs they have agreed to learn

Cost Saving Tips for your DJ or Band

- Bands are particularly open to negotiating down their costs at slow times of the year or on less popular days, like a Friday night rather than a Saturday.
- Many bands will hike up their charges if you tell them it's a wedding, so say you're calling round for quotes for a party when you first contact them.
- A daytime wedding means the band probably does not have to perform as many sets as they would in the evening, inevitably cutting down the cost. They will also be able to book an evening gig so may be more keen to discount.
- A 5-piece band will be cheaper than a 7-piece one as there are fewer musicians to pay.
- Go directly to the DJ rather than through agencies who

will take their own cut.

- Burn CDs of your favourite music to play during the meal and reserve the DJ for the dancing afterwards.
- Listen out for good DJs at clubs and bars. If they are still relatively unknown they could give you a good deal, but make sure you ask for references and check they are reliable.
- Ask a friend who's an amateur DJ to spin discs for you. If you're close to them you could even ask them to contribute their services as a wedding gift.

The First Dance

Many newlyweds are nervous about their first dance. It may help to remember that no one expects a professional dance routine. So long as you're having fun, your guests will think you look great.

Choose a piece of music you love dancing to which has special significance to you both. Pick something that is very 'you' as this will put you at ease. This may be a traditional waltz but could just as easily be an upbeat dance track. If you are having a band check well in advance that they can play the song; if you're hiring a DJ make sure they have it.

You will feel much more comfortable up there if you have put some time into practising your dance. You and your groom might like to attend a few dance lessons or even invent a routine of your own. When the moment arrives, just have fun with it and don't be afraid to laugh at yourselves if you make mistakes.

MAY I HAVE THIS DANCE?

The first dance is reserved for the newlyweds alone. What happens next is not set in stone and it's best to go with the flow on the day. Traditionally however the bride dances with her father whilst the groom dances with the bride's mother. The groom's father then cuts in to dance with the bride, whilst the bride's parents dance with each other and the groom dances with his mother. Sometimes the groom then dances with the chief bridesmaid, the bride with the best man and the in-laws dance with each other. You are then joined by the rest of the wedding party, followed by the other guests.

Popular first dance songs

I've Got You Under my Skin – Cole Porter
You're Still The One – Shania Twain
Wonderful Tonight – Eric Clapton
Underneath your Clothes – Shakira
It Must be Love – Madness
You to Me Are Everything – The Real Thing
Everything I Do (I Do it For You) – Bryan Adams
Eternal Flame – The Bangles
Come Fly With Me – Frank Sinatra
Just the Way You Are – Barry White
Can't Get Enough of Your Love – Barry White
Your Love is King – Sade
I Will Always Love You – Whitney Houston
L.O.V.E – Nat King Cole
Perfect Day – Lou Reed
My Heart Will Go On – Celine Dion
Signed, Sealed, Delivered – Stevie Wonder
The Best of My Love – The Emotions

Things Can Only Get Better – D:Ream
September – Earth, Wind and Fire
Walking on Sunshine – Katrina and the Waves
Finally (it's happened to me) – Cee Cee Peniston

A Reception without Dancing

Not keen on dancing? There are plenty of other ways to keep your guests entertained. Here are a few ideas.

- Play background music anyway as it helps people relax.
- Create a five minute slideshow featuring some of the funnier moments of you and your groom growing up.
- Ask talented guests to write a song or a sketch about you and perform it at the reception.
- Incorporate aspects of your cultural heritage by hiring traditional dancers or musicians to perform.

One Stop Review

- ☐ Choose a stunning venue with a special charm of its own.
- ☐ Create that Wow factor with decorations that continue your theme without overpowering the room's unique features.
- ☐ Use all five senses to create a special ambience.
- ☐ Choose wine and food that will be sure hits with your guests.
- ☐ Select a cake which looks **and** tastes great.
- ☐ Find reliable musicians who are passionate about your chosen music genre.
- ☐ Insist on getting all agreements in writing.

Notes

Notes

Capturing Your Day

Your wedding day itself will go by in a flash, but capturing it on film lets you relive each joyful moment any time you wish. After all when the flowers have wilted and the champagne is gone, your photographs and video will still be there to remind you of the most special day of your life.

This chapter will show you how to record your day stylishly and affordably. It will introduce you to the most popular wedding photography and video styles and reveal insider tricks on how to look great in photos. Most importantly you will learn how to choose professionals who can create timeless mementoes you are proud to display in your home.

Photography

Where do I Start?

Up until recently a bride's only photography option was that of traditional, posed bridal portraits. Now however the array of styles, effects and development techniques can be quite overwhelming. The best way to understand them is to have a brief look at where they came from.

Change is in the Air

Apart from the advent of colour film, traditional wedding photography changed very little from its origins in the 1850s until the mid 1970s. At this stage, advances in photographic technology laid the groundwork for a dramatic change in the photographic industry. A sports photojournalist in Atlanta, USA began shooting weddings in much the same way he shot football games. He created natural, unposed action shots of the day as it unfolded. This technique was named wedding photo-journalism.

The new technique excelled as a storybook description of the day, but it often failed to capture key shots like quality portraits of the bride and groom. Some photographers overcame this by posing key shots and taking a more candid approach to the rest. This method, which combines the features of the traditional and photojournalistic styles, is often referred to as the blended, modern or contemporary style.

Photography Styles Explained

Which photography style is best for you will depend on your personal preferences and the formality of your wedding. Here is a brief explanation of each.

Traditional

These are the standard, classic wedding photos we've all seen over the years which consist of artfully posed individual and group shots. While the format is standard a good photographer can achieve beautiful, timeless results.

Photojournalism or Reportage

A hot trend with today's couples, this style documents the story and feel of the day in a collection of relaxed, unposed shots. A good photojournalist will fade into the background and make themselves almost unnoticeable. The drawback is that less glamorous aspects of everyday life like scrunched up napkins or spilt wine are also captured. Many of these can be deleted later with image editing software.

Black and White

The classic, romantic look of black and white images has become increasingly popular. Many couples choose a largely black and white album accented with a few well chosen colour photographs. If you have carefully colour coordinated your day however you may prefer colour photos that capture your creation.

Cross Processing

Here slide film is processed in normal colour film chemistry to create rich, saturated colours and deep contrast. The technique works particularly well outdoors on a clear day, when the blue sky takes on a luminous quality. Similar results can be achieved by computer editing digital images.

Toned Images

You may want to have some of your wedding photographs tinted, perhaps in a sepia tone. Details of a black and white print, like the bride's bouquet, can be highlighted with hand colouring using image editing software.

Deciding on a Style

The following suggestions will help you decide what sort of look you want for your wedding photos.

Do your research

Check out the featured 'Bride of the Week' on

www.loveandcherish.net, the Real Life Weddings sections of bridal magazines and leaf through photographers' albums at wedding fairs. Browse the web and ask to see friends' wedding albums. You will soon get an idea of what you like and dislike.

Save your favourites

Save photos you particularly like in a folder and show them to any photographers you interview. They may be able to mimic some of your favourite shots, camera angles or development techniques.

Analyse your preferences

Your folder of assembled shots will tell you what sort of style you prefer. Are most of the photos in colour or black and white? Traditional or photojournalistic? Are there any special effects you admire like sepia toning, soft focus or cross processing?

One Stop Tip

Don't be tempted to ask a family member or friend to take your wedding photographs. Unless they have some sort of training you may end up with absolutely no decent mementos of your wedding day, and regret not spending the money on a professional.

Finding a Photographer

Your next step is to find a photographer who is skilled and experienced at shooting in your preferred style. Wedding magazines are a great place to look as you are exposed to a wide variety of photographic styles. You could also ask friends for recommendations or browse the internet for local photographers. Meet at least three photographers before you decide.

Look for personality

Many of us feel nervous in front of the lens, so it's important to choose someone who puts you at ease. A wedding is not the occasion for big egos or a drill-sergeant approach to arranging guests. Time constraints can make taking photos quite stressful, so choose someone who seems calm and professional under pressure. If you feel relaxed, the shoot will be more pleasant and result in better photographs. Bridal fairs give you the chance to meet lots of photographers and see who you feel most comfortable with.

Look for style

It is difficult for photographers to drastically change their style to suit yours. So if a photographer does not share your ideas of style, move on and try someone else. If it's a variety of styles you're after you can always opt to have two photographers at your wedding.

Look for consistency

A portfolio of shots from different weddings will not tell you much, as almost anyone can take the odd good picture. Instead ask to see a couple of complete wedding albums. This will show you if the photographer achieves consistently good results and if you're happy with their style.

What else to check for

When you compare several photographers' work, check who is most skilled and practised at shooting the particular style you want featured in your album. As you examine the album ask yourself the following questions:

☐ Does the album successfully tell the story of the wedding?

☐ Does it seem to capture the mood and emotions of the day and the personalities of the bride and groom?

☐ Is there a variety of pictures of the couple – some close up, some mid distance, some full length?

☐ Is the photographer creative with different poses?

☐ Is there good colour and clarity?

☐ Are the group shots tidy and well organised, and has everyone been positioned in the shot or have some been missed off at the edges?

☐ Do the pictures include close-up shots of details?

☐ Do people look relaxed and comfortable?

☐ Having met the photographer, do they seem to enjoy photographing weddings?

☐ Would you feel happy owning your version of the pictures you are shown?

One Stop Tip

Don't forget to tell your videographer and photographer of your wedding day's dress code so they can dress appropriately.

Questions for your Photographer

☐ What are their qualifications?

☐ How long they have been a photographer?

☐ Which photographic institutions are they members of?

☐ How long they have been photographing weddings?

☐ Will they personally be taking the photographs of your

wedding? If not, ask to meet the person who will be.
- ☐ Have they won any awards?
- ☐ Are they willing to travel to your venue?
- ☐ Will you be charged for travel time or is this included in the cost?
- ☐ Is the photographer familiar with your ceremony and reception location? Whilst this is not necessary, it can be helpful.
- ☐ If they have photographed your venue before, ask to see the album. Would you be happy with something similar?
- ☐ What happens in the event of bad weather?
- ☐ What are the photo package prices and how many hours do they include?
- ☐ Is the photographer willing to stay on for extra hours, and if so how much more would this cost?
- ☐ Can you buy the negatives or original digital images?
- ☐ If yes how much would this cost? If no, how many years are they kept?
- ☐ How many deposits need to be made and when would they be due?
- ☐ How much time should be built in for the formal wedding photos taken before and after the ceremony?
- ☐ What happens if they are unwell and unable to make it on the day? Do they know a good photographer who could step in if necessary?
- ☐ Do they have professional indemnity insurance to cover the cost of retaking your photographs if something goes wrong? (If not you should take out your own wedding insurance policy.)

Digital versus Film

Many professional photographers are making the switch

from film to digital. Despite early concerns over picture quality, massive advances have been made in digital technology over recent years. In fact digital cameras are now considered every bit as good as shooting on film.

Digital images are captured onto a memory card, also known as a flash card, as opposed to a roll of film. These memory cards can hold hundreds of images. They simply slot into the digital camera in place of the film roll.

Otherwise digital cameras look identical and professional cameras use exactly the same lenses. Images are shot in colour, but can later be converted to black and white or modified with other special effects using image editing software.

With a digital camera a virtually unlimited number of photographs can be taken, so there are more shots to choose from. There is, of course, no need to send the films to a photo lab for processing. This means your wedding images are available immediately and there is no risk of film being lost or damaged. Shooting digitally also allows your photographer to edit out unsightly background details like a power point on the wall behind you without first having to scan in the negative from film.

Get it in Writing

Once you have chosen your photographer, get every aspect of the agreement down in a written contract. This should include:

- ☐ Date and arrival time
- ☐ Name of the person who will photograph your wedding
- ☐ A list of all photo locations, and bad weather alternatives
- ☐ Length of shooting time
- ☐ Fees
- ☐ Overtime charges, if any

☐ A list of all locations – the bride's home, ceremony, reception etc
☐ Addresses and directions
☐ Cost of your photograph package and listed inclusions
☐ Cost of additional photos you may want to order
☐ When deposits are due
☐ Date of delivery of the final album

List your shots

With the paperwork in order, sit down with your photographer and make a list of all your 'must-have' shots. There may be particular photographs you want, like one of you and your groom being showered with confetti. If so do you mind if this is staged rather than spontaneous? Perhaps there are hand-made details that you want captured. Also list any shots you would like taken with specific guests such as old school friends or those flying in from abroad.

One Stop Tip

Inform your photographer early on if you want to send a wedding announcement and portrait to your local newspaper.

Celebrity Photo Secrets

Ever wondered how celebrities always look great in photos? Those looks may look effortless but they usually take practice and patience. It's easy to get great wedding photos with these handy insider tips.

• Spend some time in front of the mirror. Does your face look better photographed from just above or just below?

Front on or turned slightly to the side?

- Good posture is key to looking good in photos, so push your shoulders back and stand tall.
- Tan lines from shoulder straps are a no-no. If you or your bridesmaids will be exposing your shoulders try to even out your tan in the run-up to the wedding.
- Browse celebrity magazines for flattering poses and try copying them in front of the mirror.
- If you are wearing sleeves, keep your elbows pointed outwards a little so they don't look like an extension of your waistline.
- For a slimming effect on your face, turn your head slightly to the side and ask your photographer to shoot you from above.
- Carrying a white bouquet? Then include some greenery so it doesn't merge in with your dress in photographs.
- Ask your photographer to take photos an instant before the formal shots or as your guests wait to be photographed. People often look more natural and relaxed at these times and it's a great way to capture the character of the day.
- Make sure no one in the bridal party, including mums, carry items for the wedding in plastic bags, as there's nothing worse than a plastic bag lurking in the background of your photographs.

One Stop Tip

Ask your photographer to snap special wedding-day details like your dress on a hanger, the decorated reception tables or the bridesmaids' bouquets resting on a sideboard.

Cost Saving Tips for your Photographs

- Photographs will be one of your most precious keep-sakes from the day, but the best photographer for you is not necessarily the most expensive. Meet with as many as possible and trust your own judgement rather than going with the one who is most 'in' at the moment.
- Find a quality but up-and-coming photographer who is prepared to sell you the negatives or digital files as part of the package. That way you can make reprints for parents' albums or framed photos.
- Hire a photographer for just the ceremony and first hour or so of the reception.
- Scour your local photography schools for talented students with experience in wedding photography. Ask to see their portfolio and a full wedding album before you commit.

On the day

If you want photographs taken before your ceremony, begin dressing in plenty of time. One of the greatest problems photographers face is arriving at the bride's home to take the pre-wedding beauty shots, only to find the make-up artist is running late. To avoid this happening, get your hairdresser and make-up artist there early and build in at least one spare hour in case anything goes wrong.

Ask your most punctual bridesmaid to keep you updated on how much time you have left while you all get ready. If you still end up pushed for time, make sure you are made up before your bridesmaids. You should have your hair and make up finished and be ready for the photographer at least one full hour before you need to leave for the ceremony.

Wedding Video

Your groom's loving look as you walk down the aisle, the tear in your mother's eye, your father's proud speech. Who would not want these precious moments captured for all time on film?

The day itself goes past in a blur, and nothing can transport you back in time the same way as a video. There will be many amusing or endearing little details captured which, caught up in the excitement, you didn't even notice on the day itself. And whilst photographs capture key moments, only a video tells the complete story of your special day.

Videos make great mementos for family or for absent friends who could not be there. They are an investment that you can one day hand over to your children and grandchildren, allowing future generations to revisit the moment in time when you became husband and wife.

DVD OR VHS?

A DVD of your wedding will last a hundred years or more. It will be easy to make perfect copies of and will look and sound just as great in 80 years as it does today. By contrast a VHS video only lasts about twenty-five years, quality will be lost with each copy made, and the original will slowly deteriorate with each playing.

What Kind of Film?

The wedding video of yesteryear was a two or three hour record of the whole day capturing every little detail, interesting or not. Nowadays however couples demand an ever increasing level of sophistication. They usually prefer more of a documentary style, with clips edited together to create lively footage that captures the mood and feel of the day. These can include a 'highlights' video, usually about 15 minutes long, as well as a longer version.

Technological Advances

Video cameras have become significantly smaller and lighter than their predecessors. As a consequence video professionals are now much less intrusive than they once were. DVD technology allows the film to be broken down into chapters, with a feature film style menu allowing scene selection. This means you can skip to the scene you want without having to fast forward.

Telling the story

It's increasingly popular to start the movie with childhood photos and film of the bride and groom, followed by pictures of their time together. When edited together with romantic music and tasteful transitions, this effectively tells the story of how you grew up separately, met and fell in love. Some couples ask for this section to be made in advance so they can show it at their reception.

What are you paying for?

Time is money, and the two types of time you pay for in this case are shooting and production time. In terms of shooting time, the more hours spent shooting the greater the cost. Additional cameras create more interest as the same scene can be shot from different angles, but since this means doubling the number of man hours you can expect to pay more.

When it comes to production time, a good videographer can spend as much as 40 hours editing the film of a wedding together. Often this involves adding scene transitions, DVD chapters, music, special effects and end credits. The more time spent in this phase the more polished, personalised and expensive the final film will be.

Lastly you are paying for the talents of your video professional. After all, creating a production which tells the story of your day in a beautiful and creative way is an art form which comes at a price.

One Stop Tip

Check with your officiant that your ceremony venue allows video recording.

Cost Saving Tips for your Video

- The most expensive videographers are not necessarily the best. If they are new to the area they may be willing to charge less, so use wedding fairs to hunt down newbies prepared to offer special discounts.
- Choose someone who is happy to charge an hourly rate, and ask them to film just the ceremony and start of the reception.
- Ask for a shorter version of the video, for example an hour instead of the usual two. This will reduce editing time which will bring down costs.
- If you know how to use video editing software, ask if you can edit the raw footage yourself to save on production costs.
- Ask for just one cameraman instead of two.

Choosing a Videographer

Your wedding is a one shot event, so choose your videographer carefully. The best way to determine if his or her skills are up to scratch is to see samples of their work. A demo video will only show their best shots, so instead ask to see at least one full-length wedding video.

Look for crisp images, good colour and steady shots filmed with a tripod. The audio must be good – check you can hear the vows and speeches clearly. The editing should be professional with classic transitions that allow each scene to flow seamlessly into the next. Dated transitions like spin-away effects are definitely out. Widescreen is fast becoming the new standard, so it's worth asking if they have the equipment to film in native widescreen format.

The worst thing you can do when choosing a video professional is to base your decision on price alone. Find someone you like, have confidence in and whose filming style you admire. Choose someone creative who is always chasing the next shot and whose heart and soul is really in it – not someone just going through a mental tick list.

Questions for your Videographer

- ☐ How much experience do they have?
- ☐ Can you see samples of their work, including at least one full-length wedding video?
- ☐ Will they personally be filming your wedding?
- ☐ Are broadcast quality digital cameras and digital editing techniques used?
- ☐ Do they have a professional quality wireless radio microphone for the groom to wear during the ceremony, so the vows can be recorded?
- ☐ Can you provide input on how your video is edited?
- ☐ Can you choose the background music?
- ☐ Do they include a 'highlights' video?
- ☐ How long will the final film be?

- ☐ What packages are offered, what do they include and what are the prices?
- ☐ Does the price include one or two videographers?
- ☐ Can the film be supplied on DVD?
- ☐ Can it be shot in Widescreen?
- ☐ Will the final product have DVD menus and chapters?
- ☐ Is it possible to have a personalised cover and printed DVD label?
- ☐ Can you have additional copies made after the wedding?

One Stop Tip

Fortunately very few professionals will use anything but digital cameras nowadays. If you see a VHS-C camcorder, move on!

Getting it in Writing

Once you have chosen your videographer, get every aspect of the agreement down in a written contract. This should include:

- Date and arrival time
- A list of all photo locations, and bad weather alternatives
- Length of shooting time
- Fees
- Overtime charges, if any
- A list of all locations and timings – the bride's home, ceremony, reception etc
- Addresses and directions
- Cost of the package and listed inclusions
- Cost of additional videos you may want to order
- What type of equipment will be used

- When deposits are due
- Date of delivery of the final film
- Name of the person who will shoot the video
- Name of a backup videographer

One Stop Review

- ☐ Get a feel for your preferred photographic style.
- ☐ Cut cut your favourite wedding magazine photos to show to your photographer.
- ☐ Choose a photographer and videographer who will put you at ease.
- ☐ See at least one album and full-length video before you commit.
- ☐ Seek out professionals with technologically advanced equipment.
- ☐ Leave plenty of time for photos and video on the day.
- ☐ Check everything you requested is included in writing in a contract.

Notes

Notes

_____

_____

_____

_____

_____

_____

_____

_____

_____

_____

_____

_____

_____

_____

_____

_____

_____

_____

_____

_____

_____

_____

_____

_____

_____

_____

_____

Gift Registry

Your wedding is a great time to lose the hand-me-down crockery and upgrade that bedding you've had since your teens. Compiling a gift registry ensures you're given useful presents, as well as allowing each guest to breathe a sigh of relief that their gift is truly wanted.

This chapter will show you how to assemble a carefully chosen gift list that will lay the foundations for your new life together, so at least at the outset of marriage, everything in your household matches everything else.

Where do I Start?

Your first decision is which shops to register with. Many stores promote a 'gift registry service', which allows you to record a list of their products that you would like to receive. When a friend buys an item from the list it is removed, so you never receive any item twice.

Department stores offer a stress-free environment for compiling your list. The selection is varied, they are open after hours and there's probably a café where you can take a break. Often the store will include a gift which you receive just for hosting your registry with them.

Whilst most brides simply register with one or two department stores, if you need something specific like kitchen items or soft furnishings you might want to register with a speciality shop. If some guests have long distances to travel, think about using an online registry or a department store with shops in different locations.

> ## One Stop Tip
> Be sure to select more gifts than the number of guests invited so everyone has plenty of choice.

Gift registry questions

- ☐ Does the store stock a wide variety of items in designs or patterns you like?
- ☐ Do they deliver?
- ☐ Are their branches conveniently located in other cities for out of towners, and if so are internet or phone orders possible?
- ☐ What is their returns and exchange policy?
- ☐ What happens if an item is delivered damaged?

Consider registering with several services

You are not bound to one store when it comes to gift registries – in fact it's worthwhile seeking out perhaps two that fulfil different needs. You might want to set up a honeymoon gift registry through your travel agent, or open up a new bank account and ask for contributions towards a deposit on a home.

Compile your list

Once you have chosen which stores to register with you will need to compile your list. It's easy to get carried away with all the great products, so list what you actually need in advance. You can use the pre-assembled Gift List Suggestions at the end of this chapter and tick off the items you want.

Hit the shops

Now you have an idea of what you actually need, take your Gift List Suggestions to the stores you have chosen to register with. They will provide you with a form to fill in, or possibly a PDA with a barcode scanner. Simply find each product you want, pick the model you like best, and record this on the store's form or PDA.

WHAT TO CHOOSE

A well assembled gift registry will strike a good balance between practical items you need, and luxury products you want. Select items from a broad price range so guests of varying incomes can afford to buy you something. This means not only should you list cheaper items, but also more expensive gifts that close family or wealthier friends may want to buy you.

Gift Registry Etiquette

Registry Cards

Many bridal registries provide cards announcing that you are registered with their store that can be enclosed with each guest's invitation. This is great for the department store as it increases the likelihood of your guests buying from them, but including registry details with invitations is traditionally an etiquette no-no. For a more detailed discussion of this constantly evolving aspect of wedding etiquette, see 'Including gift registry details' in the Stationery chapter.

Returning Gifts

Even if you have a gift registry, duplicate gifts do occasionally occur. If this happens it is better not to tell the guest who sent it that you returned their particular gift.

One Stop Tip

Always remember it's perfectly acceptable for a guest to buy you something that's not on the list.

Broken or Damaged Gifts

If you do your homework and only register with stores that have good returns policies, broken or damaged gifts should not be much of a problem. Simply contact the store's customer service department and they will see that a replacement is sent.

Any damaged electrical goods are likely to be covered by warranty, so contact the gift giver and get the details so it can be exchanged. Otherwise, unless the gift was sent insured there is probably not much that can be done. It's up to you whether or not you mention that the gift arrived broken. Bear in mind however that if you do, the giver may feel guilty and obligated to buy you another.

Keeping Track of Gifts

You will need to know who gave you which gift when you write your thank you letters, so it's important to record each gift you receive and who gave it to you. Use the Gift Recorder at the end of this chapter, and fill it in as each gift arrives.

Thank you letters

Writing your thank you notes is the one task that you can not delegate. These should be hand written from you and your groom, mentioning the specific gift you received. It's polite to write one thank you note for each gift you get, whether it is from the bridal shower, engagement party or wedding. Thank you notes should ideally be sent out within two weeks for gifts received before your wedding. As for presents which arrive after your big day, it's best to write thank yous for these within one month of your wedding – although up to three months is fine.

GETTING IT DELIVERED

Most registries offer gift-wrapping and home delivery services. These allow you to request a date for the gifts to be delivered so they all come at once. Many couples like to schedule this for a few days after they return from their honeymoon, so they can look forward to unwrapping their presents when they arrive home.

Gift Registry Checklist

Dinnerware	Store	Quantity
Casserole dish		
Fruit bowl		
Salad bowl		
Serving bowl		
Salad servers		
Gravy boat		
Teapot		
Coffee pot		
Sugar bowl		
Salt and pepper set		
Cake plate		

Dinnerware continued	Store	Quantity
Butter dish		
Serving spoons/fork		
Butter knife		
Serving tray		
Dips platter		
8 to 12 of the following:		
Dinner plates		
Dessert plates		
Side plates		
Soup / cereal bowls		
Pasta/soup bowls		
Cups and saucers		

Table Linen	Store	Quantity
Tablecloth		
8 to 12 of the following:		
Place mats		
Napkins		
Napkin rings		

Crystal and Glassware	Store	Quantity
Pitcher		
Cocktail shaker		
Wine rack		
Ice bucket and tongs		
8 to 12 of the following:		
Red wineglasses		
White wineglasses		
Water glasses		
Champagne flutes		
Iced beverage glasses		
Beer mugs		
Cocktail glasses		
Irish coffee glasses		

Cookware	Store	Quantity
Saucepan set		

Frying pan		
Non-stick pan		
Griddle		
Grill pan		
Steamer		
Double boiler		
Kettle		
Roasting dish		
Casserole dish		
Microwave cookware set		
Wok		

Bakeware	Store	Quantity
Baking tray		
Cake pan		
Loaf pan		
Pie pan		
Muffin pan		
Mixing bowl set		
Rolling pin		
Measuring cups		
Pizza pan		

Kitchen Appliances	Store	Quantity
Toaster		
Blender		
Microwave oven		
Coffee maker		
Coffee grinder		
Food processor		
Hand mixer		
Bread maker		
Pasta maker		
Rice maker		
Waffle maker		
Steamer		
Electric can opener		
Juicer		

Cutlery	Store	Quantity
Cutlery set		
Knife block		
Bread knife		
Paring knife		
Utility knife		
Set of steak knives		
Sharpening steel		
Kitchen shears		
Cutting board		

Kitchen (other)	Store	Quantity
Spice rack		
Dish cloths		
Pot holders		
Apron		
Storage jars		
Cheese board		

Bedroom (specify standard, queen or king size)	Store	Quantity
Flat sheets		
Fitted sheets		
Pillowcases		
Pillows		
Pillow shams		
Bed spread		
Bed skirts		
Duvet		
Duvet cover		
Lightweight blanket		
Heavy blanket		
Quilt		
Mattress pad		

Bathroom	Store	Quantity
Bath towels		
Hand towels		

Wash cloths		
Guest towels		
Bath mat		
Bathroom scale		

Home Décor	Store	Quantity
Vase		
Picture frame		
Decorative bowl		
Candlesticks/candle holders		
Clock		
Lamp		
Framed art		

Luggage	Store	Quantity
Suitcases (specify sizes)		
Carry-on luggage		
Beauty case		

Electronics	Store	Quantity
Stereo		
VCR/DVD Player		
Camcorder		
Camera		
Camera accessories		
Telephone		
Clock radio		

Other	Store	Quantity
Vacuum cleaner		
Iron		
Wine cooler		
Picnic hamper		
His and hers dressing gowns		
Tools		
Furniture		
Patio and outdoor furniture		
Barbeque		

Sports or fitness gear		
Travel or camping gear		
Books – specify titles		
Additional		

Gift Recorder

Name	Gift description	Date received	Thank you sent?

Name	Gift description	Date received	Thank you sent?

Name	Gift description	Date received	Thank you sent?

Name	Gift description	Date received	Thank you sent?

One Stop Review

☐ Pick one or more quality stores to register with.

☐ Tick off the items you would like on the above list.

☐ Take this list to the store(s) you have registered with and choose the products you like.

☐ Select more gifts than the number of guests invited so there is plenty of choice.

☐ Record gifts received in the Gift Recorder above.

☐ Send timely, personalised, hand written thank you notes as gifts arrive.

Notes

_____

_____

_____

_____

_____

_____

_____

_____

_____

_____

_____

_____

_____

_____

_____

_____

_____

_____

_____

_____

_____

_____

_____

_____

_____

_____

_____

Notes

Bridal Beauty Secrets

Every bride dreams of gliding down the aisle happy, radiant and beautiful to her spellbound groom. And with the right health and beauty know-how, that dream can become a reality.

Glowing skin, shiny hair and a lovely smile are not exclusive to Hollywood stars. The secret is to start a beauty routine as early as possible and stick with it right up to your big day. This chapter will show you all you need to know to achieve a flawless, glowing complexion, healthy hair and a dazzling smile.

Where do I start?

Begin by listing any treatments you know you will need such as facials, haircuts or manicures. Book these appointments now so you get into a routine of looking after yourself.

If you want to lose a few pounds, begin your weight loss programme as soon as possible. Start by making an appointment with your doctor, nutritionist or a personal trainer. These professionals will be able to motivate you throughout your journey and advise you on the best way to reach your personal goals.

Any skin conditions such as eczema or acne need to be addressed early on, as skin treatments like as micro-dermabrasion can take up to three months to achieve results. You'll also want a great smile, so make a trip to the dentist immediately to check for any problems. Schedule your last scale and polish shortly before your wedding day.

Skincare

Makeup can do a lot of things, but whatever anyone tells you it can not create flawless skin. For a bright, luminous complexion you need to look after yourself both inside and out.

Start a skincare routine

Start a skincare regime as soon as possible. Department stores offer free skincare consultations, so visit several counters at a quiet time and ask for advice. Discuss any skin problems you have and find quality products which feel good and suit your skin type. Cleansing, toning and moisturising your skin morning and night will keep it smooth, healthy and blemish free.

Exfoliate regularly

Exfoliate to remove dead skin cells and keep your skin supple and smooth. Use a cleanser with exfoliating granules on your face twice a week, and on your body once a week.

Modify your diet

What we eat and drink plays a vital part in the health of our skin. For a glowing complexion you will need to up your fruit and vegetable intake and cut back on sugar, processed and fatty foods. Dull, lifeless skin is usually due to dehydration. To combat this drink at least eight 250ml glasses of water a day and avoid coffee, black tea, caffeinated soft drinks and alcohol.

This will soon flush toxins out of your system, leaving your skin looking fresh and plump.

Wear sunscreen

Sun exposure is damaging even if you don't burn as it leaves skin looking dull, patchy and encourages premature wrinkles. Use sunscreen religiously before your wedding, especially on your face, neck and chest area. If you live in a hot climate opt for nothing lower than SPF 30; otherwise SPF 15 should be fine.

Fake it

Last minute tanning sessions can go horribly awry – and the last thing you want on your wedding day is a sunburnt face or peeling nose! If you want a tanned look, choose a professional fake tan treatment. Find a product which will not rub off and stain your dress and remember to exfoliate thoroughly before applying. If in doubt, head for a beauty salon and get it professionally applied. Arrange your final application a couple of days before your wedding.

One Stop Tip

Want smooth, kissable lips? Then use a toothbrush every night to gently exfoliate them and remove any dry skin.

Overcoming acne

The number one skin complaint from brides is acne. If this is a problem for you, start treating it as soon as possible. Mild breakouts can be controlled with products containing pore-cleansing benzoyl peroxide or alpha-hydroxy acids, both available over the counter from most pharmacists. Your doctor may be able to prescribe a contraceptive pill which can improve your skin, but you should ideally start taking it at least six months before your big day.

Skin clinics can treat acne conditions with micro-dermabrasion, a relatively new technique to smooth and resurface the skin. This is a safe, painless treatment which usually eradicates acne within three months. A machine is used to cleanse the skin, emptying out blocked pores with a gentle vacuuming action. Then a fine jet of aluminium oxide crystals are sprayed onto the area, smoothing it and removing dead skin cells.

One Stop Tip

Detoxing tends to give you spots, so complete any detox diet a few months before the big day.

Getting in Shape

Every bride wants to walk down the aisle looking slim and stunning. While we can't wave a magic wand, proper diet and exercise will certainly help you look and feel your best on the day and throughout your married life.

Set realistic goals

You don't want to stress yourself out before your wedding day with a gruelling regimen, so start by setting yourself realistic targets. Concentrate on a routine of healthy eating and regular exercise rather than dieting. Increased exercise can actually add weight because of increased muscle, so measure your waistline to check your progress as well as weighing yourself.

Make exercise a habit

Do at least half an hour of cardiovascular exercise that

you enjoy, three times or more a week. It might be swimming, working out at the gym, brisk walking to and from work, inline skating or cycling. Alternatively why not take a dance class? As well as being fun and healthy, the moves you learn will make you look good during your first dance. Anything that gets your heart rate up so you're slightly out of breath will help you shed weight. Increased fitness will also make you feel healthier and more relaxed in the run-up to your wedding.

EXERCISE FOR THE BUSY BRIDE

It can be hard for the working bride to find time for exercise, so why not incorporate it into your daily routine? Brisk walking is great for burning off calories. Get off the bus a few stops early, go for a walk during your lunch break, take the stairs instead of the escalator or walk the dog. Choose hilly terrain and take it easy to start with, building up to a faster pace over a period of days. You may want to monitor your progress with a pedometer, which measures how many steps you take.

Eating Healthily

- Use visualisation to motivate yourself. Spend a few minutes each day picturing yourself as slim and gorgeous in your wedding dress.
- Drink a glass of water with lemon juice on waking to kick-start your metabolism, and don't eat anything else for twenty minutes.
- Eat plenty of fruit and vegetables.
- Eat lots of high-protein foods such as meat, fish and poultry.
- Foods which advertise 'fat free' on the packaging are often loaded with sugar, so check the label.

- Drinking plenty of water throughout the day will help keep you feeling full. Thirst is often mistaken for hunger so always drink water before eating a meal.
- Grill or roast food rather than frying.
- Trim off visible fat and remove the skin from chicken and turkey.
- Eat slowly and stop when you're full.
- Lose weight slowly and steadily, aiming for a 1-2lbs (up to 1 kilogram) per week.
- Eat little and often to stave off the hunger pangs. This will keep your blood sugar levels even which helps avoid cravings.
- A little of what you fancy is fine. Small amounts of chocolate won't slow your weight loss if you resist the urge to binge.
- Don't weigh yourself more than once a week – it's demoralising!

One Stop Tip

When it comes to pre-wedding hair removal, waxing is the best option. It gives the smoothest finish of all and will keep you hair-free throughout your honeymoon.

Hair Care

To get your hair into tip-top condition for the big day, start looking after it as soon as you are engaged. Leave it to dry naturally as often as possible, avoid curling irons or straighteners and get a haircut every six to eight weeks. If you have dry or bleached hair ask for a deep conditioning treatment each time you visit the hairdresser's – the results will amaze you.

Colouring

For your wedding day, colouring is definitely best left to the professionals. Experiment with a new colour well before the big day so you have time to change it if it doesn't quite work. You can't go wrong with natural looking, subtle highlights which compliment your skin tone and highlight your eyes.

Choosing your Wedding Hairstyle

The texture and look of your wedding gown can help you decide on a hairstyle. The smooth, shiny up-do matches a sleek satin gown, whereas a pretty tulle skirt will be complimented by soft, tumbling curls.

Face Shape

If you have a long face, avoid styles which are piled on top of your head and try to add width. The bride with a strong jaw or round face should steer clear of anything which adds width, and instead create height with a loose or neat up-do. Brides with heart-shaped faces can add width at the chin with layers or a blunt bob.

Long Hair

If a ponytail compliments your face shape, an elegant up-do will probably suit you. If you look better with your hair worn down, try wearing half of it up with the rest falling around your shoulders. Wearing it all down can also look natural and romantic if it's well styled. Incorporate unique details from your dress by twisting or braiding your hair to echo the weave of the fabric, or thread pearls or crystals through to match those on your bodice.

Medium Hair

Medium length hair looks great curled with heated rollers to give it extra volume, then topped with a sparkling tiara or decorated with sparkly hair clips. With the help of a good stylist you can also wear it up. You can add volume with a 'doughnut', a piece of net-covered sponge. This is positioned on the crown of the head and the hair is pinned around it to add height.

Short Hair

Get a really good cut just before your wedding day. Back-comb your hair slightly if you need to add volume or use a curling iron, curling your hair away from the face and adding height on the crown of your head. Leave your hair until it cools and, if you want to add texture, run some wax through it and define the odd curl. Use a tiara to dress it up, dot it with fresh flower buds or add some hair jewels.

DIY STYLING

If you decide to style your own hair, make sure you get plenty of practice in. You should try fixing your headdress and veil firmly to your head with bobby pins so it does not come off half way through the day.

At the hairdresser's

Meet your hairdresser well in advance to discuss what kind of hairstyle you want. Arrange a free consultation at a quiet time when you will not be rushed.

Your consultation

This is the time to tell your hairdresser as much as possible about your wedding, including the style of dress and formality of the day. Show your hairdresser pictures from magazines, tell them any ideas you have for your hair and then ask for suggestions. If you like what they say you can book a trial, which you will have to pay for.

Your trial

Bring your headdress and veil along to your practice session. This is the time to iron out any concerns you may have, so don't be shy to ask for aspects of the style to be changed. Having your bridesmaid or Mum on hand will give you moral support and a trusted second opinion.

Booking your appointment

Happy with the result? Then ask your hairdresser to make detailed notes about the style. You will need to decide whether you want to visit the salon on your wedding day or get the hairdresser to come to your house. Whatever you choose, ask for the booking in writing.

THE EYES HAVE IT

Well-shaped eyebrows will widen your eyes and balance your features, but beware of the temptation to overpluck. Why not have your eyebrows professionally waxed by a beautician a few days before your wedding? If you're fair skinned you may also want to have your eyelashes and eybrows tinted at your hairdressers'.

Nails

Your hands will be the focus of much attention on your wedding day as you show off your new ring. To keep your hands and nails in good condition get into the habit of using a hand cream every day and giving yourself a manicure once a week.

To finish off, get a professional manicure the day before your wedding. A French manicure or very faint shimmer is the way to go – anything more will draw attention away from your ring.

Makeup

Your wedding day makeup should enhance your best features so you look like a better version of yourself. Chances are you already have a good idea of what suits you. So if you're not really a dark lipstick kind of girl, go with what feels right and choose a shade you're more comfortable with.

Take your cue from your dress. Soft, feminine colours go with a soft, floaty dress whereas a chic, glamorous gown suits a more dramatic look. Use the hue of your dress as inspiration, picking up pink or silver tones in your makeup. Golds and peachy tones work well with ivory dresses, whilst cooler plum shades suit bright white gowns.

Brunettes usually suit warm colours with eye makeup in cream, browns, gold and copper and lips in rich tones of burgundy or plum. Darker complexions can take more vibrant colours like fuchsia, raspberry and wine. If your skin is black or deep olive, stay away from pastels as they can make you look washed out. Dark grey is best avoided, especially on olive skin.

Fair blondes with cool skin undertones should try eye makeup in shades of blue, white, pink and lavender. Lips look luscious in dusky rose or pinkish plum colours. Avoid deep, dull colours like olive, khaki and dark plums.

Blondes with warmer complexions best suit neutral

colours with peachy undertones, but should steer clear of bright colours. Try shades of cream or golden brown with lips painted in plum, ginger-brown or warm red.

Redheads look good in earthy tones like terracotta, copper, peach and moss green. For lips, try peachy shades or brick red. Redheads with auburn hair should avoid pastel colours, whilst those with white skin and carrot red hair should steer clear of orange, bluish reds and fuchsia.

If in doubt stick to soft, neutral colours as they enhance the complexion and flatter any skin tone.

Cost Saving Tips

- Ask a glamorous friend to do your makeup and / or hair. Just make sure you schedule plenty of practice sessions with her before your wedding day.
- Go to your salon. This is usually cheaper than getting a hair and makeup artist to come to you.
- If your mother and bridesmaids are being made up, negotiate a discounted rate with your makeup artist.
- Apply your own makeup. If your skills aren't up to scratch, get a free lesson at a department store cosmetic counter. You can apply what you learn to cheaper cosmetics, but leave space in your budget for a quality foundation which closely matches your skin tone. Practise your look plenty of times before the big day, check how it looks in photos and get feedback from friends or family.
- Ask your bridesmaids, mother and your fiancé's mother to pay for their own makeup if they want it done professionally.

Why choose a Makeup artist?

Your wedding day makeup needs to make you look stunning on the day, great in the photos and still stay put until the end of the night. That's a tall order for most of us!

To look good in photos you'll need a look which is slightly stronger than usual. However a deep lipstick which works well in real life can look gothic in photographs. A very light lipstick on the other hand can make you look pale and washed out.

Foundation can also be a problem. If it contains the common ingredient titanium dioxide your skin may look great in real life, but appear several shades lighter in photographs which use flash.

A makeup artist will be experienced in balancing these issues by choosing the right products and using tips and tricks to make you look great on the day.

Questions for your makeup artist

- ☐ Is there availability on your wedding day?
- ☐ What is the pricing structure, and what does it include?
- ☐ Which extras would incur additional costs, eg false eyelashes?
- ☐ What are the travel costs?
- ☐ Are they formally trained?
- ☐ What experience do they have?
- ☐ Can you see a portfolio of their previous work?
- ☐ Are discounts available if the bridesmaids and your Mum also have their makeup done?

One Stop Tip

Doing your own makeup? Artists' brushes work just as well as makeup brushes and are a lot cheaper.

Your practice session

A good makeup artist will be able to create just the look you desire, be it glamorous, romantic, natural or seductive. Look at their portfolio of previous work to see how flexible they are at achieving different looks. Choose someone who puts you at ease and you feel understands the kind of look you want. If you like their style, book an appointment for a trial.

You may want to bring your mother or a bridesmaid along to your practice session for a second opinion. You will need to describe exactly what sort of look you want, so take along magazine photos. It's also helpful to wear something of a similar colour to that of your wedding gown. Don't be shy about asking the makeup artist to change something or to try a different look – after all, that's what a trial is all about.

One Stop Tip

To get a good idea of how your wedding look will come together, book your hair and makeup trial for the same day.

DIY Makeup

Many brides choose to do their own makeup, and with a little guidance and lots of practice the results can be great. Bear in mind however that the cost of buying quality cosmetics can quickly begin to rival that of hiring a makeup artist.

Hit the makeup counters

Start by having a few makeovers at the makeup counters in department stores. These are usually free or very cheap and are a great way to discover which colours suit your skin tone. Try to wear something the same colour as your wedding dress, and ask the staff to demonstrate how it's applied so you can copy the technique yourself.

Keep it matte

When it comes to foundation there's a place for the 'dewy' look – and it's not at your wedding! It may look fresh and natural in real life but in photographs your skin will just look greasy, so play it safe and finish with a dusting of loose powder for a matt complexion. Also bear in mind that matte eye shadows last longer and look better in photos than frosted ones. Dark shades can look a little harsh, so stick to light or medium eye shadow and blend well.

Practice makes perfect

Once you have the cosmetics you need, start practising applying them. You may want to ask a friend to take a photograph of you to check your look works well in photographs. At this stage there's still time for fine-tuning.

On the day

Wedding day makeup should be a little more intense than usual, as if you are going to a black tie dinner. Start by applying an oil-free moisturiser over your face. Make sure the eye area is not overly moisturised as this will cause your eye makeup to crease. Smoothing on an eye makeup primer afterwards will help your eye makeup stay put.

Foundation

Next apply foundation all over your face including your eyelids, smoothing on just enough to achieve even coverage. Cover any dark under eye circles by patting concealer from the inside corner of your eye next to your nose to the middle of your under eye area. Don't extend it any further or it will emphasize any crow's feet or fine lines.

LAYING GOOD FOUNDATIONS

Foundation is a vital part of every bride's makeup kit as it helps smooth out the skin tone and hide imperfections. Be very careful about the foundation you buy. It should match your skin tone exactly. Custom-blended foundations, like those by Prescriptives sold at department store cosmetic counters, are well worth the investment even if they are slightly more expensive. Alternatively you could try one of the many new optical illusion foundations such as those by Lancome which refract light for a soft, glowing look. Whatever you choose make sure you check the effect in natural light, even if it means stepping out of the shop to look at yourself in daylight in your compact.

Blusher

Cream blusher lasts longer than the powder variety – just make sure you use it sparingly and blend well. It can however be a little tricky to apply, so if you are not comfortable using it stick with the powder variety. Use a large brush to apply powder blusher to your cheekbones, blending upwards.

Eyes

Start with a pale eye shadow. Choose from almost white to bone or peach, depending on your skin tone. Apply it from lash line to brow. Layer a medium shade over it from lash line to just above the eye socket crease, blending well. Line your top lashes with a soft black pencil, or brown for a softer look. Use a very thin brush to smudge a deep eye shadow in a matching shade over your eye liner for a soft, smoky look rather than a harsh line. Curl your lashes three times, then apply volumizing waterproof mascara to your top lashes only.

Lips

To make lipstick last start by lining your lips with a lip pencil. Apply lipstick with a brush, then blot with a thin piece of tissue. Leave the tissue on your lips and press a powder puff on top of the tissue to seal it. Remove the tissue and reapply your lipstick and lip liner, blending with a lip brush. For extra glamour apply a little gloss, but go easy as too much will reflect in the photographs.

And to finish...

To set your makeup apply loose powder all over your face and neck. Honey or yellow toned powder works best, as translucent powder can make your face look pale in flash photographs.

TOUCH UP KIT

Put together a touch up kit for your wedding day. Every bride should keep powder handy to maintain a matte finish on her face for photos as well as lipstick, blusher, a comb, tissues and safety pins. Ask one of your bridesmaids to carry it for you in her handbag.

Dealing with Wedding Stress

Since ancient times the bride has been celebrated as the embodiment of beauty, goodness and serenity, but when you're running around frantically trying to get everything done, that can be pretty tough to live up to.

There's no doubt that you will feel stressed at some time during the planning of your wedding. Symptoms can include feeling tense, excited, nervous or tearful. You may have trouble sleeping, be short tempered or feel generally overwhelmed. And if you are getting little sleep, skipping meals or feeling stressed, it's difficult to look your best.

Planning your wedding does not have to be worrying if you take the time to relax and enjoy the experience. The fact is that things will go wrong, but you will probably not even notice on the day. Once you accept that not everything will turn out exactly as planned, things will start to seem less stressful. Here are some other techniques you can use to help yourself feel calmer.

Eat well

Eat a balanced diet that includes plenty of fruit, vegetables and wholegrain foods. Up your intake of fish, bananas and leafy vegetables – all natural stress relievers. Too much caffeine is known to raise stress levels, so drink less black tea, coffee and caffeinated soft drinks.

Get moving

Studies show frequent aerobic exercise reduces stress by relaxing tense muscles and triggering the brain's feel-good chemicals, known as endorphins. Choose activities you enjoy which leave you slightly out of breath like dancing, swimming or walking. Aim to work out at least three times a week.

Sleep soundly

Make sure you get enough hours of sleep. If you're having trouble nodding off take a hot bath and avoid tea, coffee or alcohol before bedtime. Instead choose something relaxing like camomile tea or a mug of hot milk.

Delegate

Your wedding is the one time in your life when everyone is only too happy to help arrange things. If you're feeling over-whelmed, ask for help and it will be gladly given.

Give each other space

Arrange to spend some time apart with friends, family or on your own. When you are reunited with your fiancé you will feel refreshed and appreciate each other more.

Use natural stress-busters

Many natural remedies are thought to help reduce stress. Try the Australian Bushflower Emergency Essence or Bach Flower Rescue Remedy, both of which can help in times of stress. You may also wish to visit a natropath, who can mix up a highly effective customised herbal remedy for you.

Spoil yourself

Leave it to the professionals and treat yourself to a massage, reiki, acupuncture, meditation, or listen to relaxation tapes. Or why not plan a trip to a spa?

Focus on each other

Making time to plan the rest of your lives together will help you see your relationship as continuous, rather than culminating in just one day. Have fun together, do hobbies you both enjoy or get away for a long weekend.

Communicate

Share your problems with each other and try to resolve them together. Spend time talking about things other than your wedding to put things into perspective.

One Stop Review

- ☐ Start a skin and hair care routine early and follow it right up to your wedding day.
- ☐ Visit the dentist and address problem skin conditions as soon as possible.
- ☐ Make exercise and healthy eating a habit.
- ☐ Choose a hairstyle that suits your face shape, and makeup that compliments your skin.
- ☐ Get plenty of sleep and don't skip meals.
- ☐ Use stress busting techniques to stay calm.

Notes

Notes

Honeymoon

Planning your first holiday as husband and wife is, for most couples, one of the most exciting parts of arranging the wedding. In this chapter you will discover how you can make this holiday of a lifetime just the romantic, unforgettable experience you have always dreamed of.

Where do I Start?

Whether you want luxury, sightseeing or adventure, a reliable travel agent should be your first stop. Visit them at a quiet time and describe every detail of your dream honeymoon. They will be able to recommend all sorts of spectacular destinations to fit your requirements – and your budget.

The Internet is another great source of ideas. There are plenty of travel and honeymooner forums where you can get insider tips and advice from people who have travelled to your chosen destination. You might also like to browse the travel section in your local bookshop.

One Stop Tip

You'll be exhausted after your wedding so even if you're in to adventure holidays, plan in a few days relaxation time.

Don't forget...

- ☐ Get your inoculations well in advance.
- ☐ Purchase medications you will need such as malaria tablets or contraceptive pills.
- ☐ Ask your travel agent if you need a visa.
- ☐ Book your honeymoon tickets under your maiden name so it matches your passport and driver's license.
- ☐ Take out travel insurance to protect you against unforeseen events like your luggage being lost or one of you getting ill (your travel agent will be able to advise you on this).

SURPRISE!

Traditionally it's the groom's job to organise, book and pay for the honeymoon, often keeping the destination a secret from the bride. Nowadays however most couples choose to plan the trip together so they can be sure it's the kind of holiday they will both enjoy. If you like the element of surprise you could choose to shortlist a few destinations together, but leave the final choice up to your groom.

Ramp up the romance

There are many thoughtful little ways to make your honeymoon extra special, so get creative. Here are a few romantic ideas.

- Choose a hotel in a romantic setting, perhaps overlooking a picturesque lake or deserted beach.
- Request a secluded room with a view, spa bath or four poster bed.
- Pack some sensual items like massage oil, romantic

music or candles.

- Tell your hotel and airline you are newlyweds when you book, and pack a copy of your marriage certificate as proof. You may find you receive special treatment like a bottle of champagne or an upgrade to business class.

- Your honeymoon is the perfect excuse to splash out, so do something that you wouldn't do on a normal holiday. Get that room upgrade or limousine transfer, take that sunset cruise, book a massage for two or indulge in a helicopter ride.

- Be impulsive – go for a moonlit walk, ride in a horse drawn carriage or order champagne when the mood takes you.

- Remember to bring home a special memento from your trip.

One Stop Tip

If possible, don't fly out the day after your wedding. You will probably need the day to relax and wind down from all the excitement before getting on a plane.

Affording It

Do you have your heart set on a honeymoon you can't afford? If so you could consider a honeymoon gift registry where your friends and family can make donations to your trip of a lifetime.

Postponing your trip is another option. This will give you something to look forward to after all the excitement of the wedding has died down. It's probably also a better solution than taking out a loan and starting married life with money worries.

> ## One Stop Tip
> Before your wedding day make sure you put your airline tickets, hotel confirmation and passports in a place where you won't forget them.

Cost Saving Tips

- Use any Frequent Flyer points you've accumulated from wedding expenses paid for with your credit card.
- Holiday somewhere closer to home to cut your travel costs, so you can splurge on accommodation and have more spending money.
- Often packages which include flights, accommodation and meals can be the best value.
- Ask guests to buy honeymoon vouchers instead of wedding gifts. They can either pay money into a specially set up honeymoon bank account, or buy you flight vouchers from the airline you'll be travelling with.

Honeymoon Essentials

- ☐ Passports and visas
- ☐ Tickets
- ☐ Money
- ☐ Reservation information (hotel, rental car, etc)
- ☐ Travel itinerary
- ☐ Traveller's cheques
- ☐ List of traveller's cheque numbers (keep separate from cheques) – consider leaving a copy with a friend
- ☐ Travel insurance
- ☐ Medication
- ☐ Emergency phone numbers
- ☐ Driver's licenses

- ☐ Hand wipes
- ☐ Tissues
- ☐ Keys for luggage, car and house
- ☐ Eyewear

Clothing

- ☐ Underwear
- ☐ Shoes and sandals
- ☐ Socks and tights
- ☐ Shirts and tops
- ☐ Trousers
- ☐ Pullovers
- ☐ One smart outfit each
- ☐ Dresses
- ☐ Swimwear
- ☐ Umbrella
- ☐ Coat or jacket
- ☐ Hat
- ☐ Gloves
- ☐ Nightwear
- ☐ Belts
- ☐ Jewellery

Toiletries

- ☐ Shampoo and conditioner
- ☐ Razors and shaving cream
- ☐ Soap
- ☐ Moisturiser
- ☐ Makeup
- ☐ Hairbrush or comb
- ☐ Toothpaste
- ☐ Toothbrushes

- [ ] Dental floss
- [ ] Nail clippers and nail file
- [ ] Deodorant
- [ ] Contraception (if needed)
- [ ] Over-the-counter medication (aspirin, antacids, re-hydration salts etc.)
- [ ] Vitamins
- [ ] Contact lens solution
- [ ] Sunscreen
- [ ] After sun lotion
- [ ] Insect repellent
- [ ] Feminine hygiene products
- [ ] Hair dryer
- [ ] Curling iron

Miscellaneous

- [ ] Camera, film and batteries
- [ ] Video camera
- [ ] Glasses or contact lenses
- [ ] Sun glasses
- [ ] Alarm clock
- [ ] Corkscrew
- [ ] Binoculars
- [ ] First aid kit
- [ ] Needle and thread
- [ ] Maps
- [ ] Books and magazines

One Stop Review

- ☐ Decide what sort of trip you want, then visit your travel agent.
- ☐ Plan in some relaxation time.
- ☐ Think of little ways to make your honeymoon extra special.
- ☐ Take out travel insurance.
- ☐ Broadcast your newlywed status – you may get special treatment.
- ☐ Pack early and use the Honeymoon Essentials checklist so you don't forget anything.

Notes

Notes

Glossary of Bridal Terms

A-line

A style of dress that is fitted through the bodice with a slightly flared skirt.

American Style

A popular style of modern wedding cake where tiers are stacked directly on top of each other rather than supported by pillars.

Arm Sheaf

A bouquet made to be cradled in one arm.

Ascot Tie

A wide type of necktie that is reserved for the most formal of daytime weddings, and worn with a morning suit.

Ballet

Also known as a waltz, this veil length drops below the bride's knees but above her ankles.

Ballgown

A style of gown which has a fitted bodice and a very full skirt.

Basket Weave

Decorative piping on the wedding cake which features inter-linked horizontal and vertical lines of icing.

Bateau

A high neckline which curves down slightly below the collar bone.

Biedermeier

A posy where different coloured flowers are arranged in rings according to their colour (see *Posy*).

Blusher

A single layered shoulder length veil.

Bomboniere

An Italian term for 'favours', gifts which are given to wedding guests as a keepsake to thank them for their attendance.

Boutonniere

A tiny flower arrangement usually worn by the groom, best man, groomsmen and the male relatives of the bride and groom. It is worn over the heart on the left lapel of the jacket.

Bow Tie

The most popular choice of tie to wear with a tuxedo.

Bridal Procession

The aisle walk which marks the start of the wedding ceremony where the bride, on her father's arm, walks down the aisle accompanied by her entourage.

Bridal Shower

A pre-wedding party traditionally hosted and organised by the chief bridesmaid, where the bride and groom are 'showered' with gifts for their new home.

Butter cream

A soft, creamy icing that can be coloured, flavoured and used in the decoration or filling of a wedding cake.

Buttonhole

See *boutonniere.*

Bun wrap

A band that encircles an up-do type hairstyle.

Calligraphy

An ornate, stylized form of handwriting seen on some wedding invitations.

Cascade

See *Shower.*

Cathedral

The longest of veils, reaching to the floor with a slight train.

Chapel

A bridal veil which reaches to the floor.

Chief Bridesmaid

See *Maid Of Honour.*

Columns

See *Pillars.*

Comb

An alternative to the tiara, this headpiece has long comb-like teeth.

Composite Bouquet

A handmade bouquet where different petals or buds are wired together on a single stem, creating the illusion of one giant flower.

Corsage

An arrangement of flowers worn by female relatives of the bride and groom to mark them out as special. The corsage is usually pinned to the bodice of a dress or jacket.

Crown

A fully circular bead-adorned head piece which is larger than both a half crown and tiara.

Cummerbund

A broad, pleated sash of silk or satin worn around a man's waist on top of his shirt, covering the trousers' waistband. Usually black but may be any colour.

Dais

A platform raised from the floor where the bride and groom are seated in some wedding receptions.

Damask

A fabric with raised patterns woven into it similar to brocade, but heavier.

Digital Printing

The least expensive wedding stationery printing option with results similar to those of offset printing. See the *Stationery* chapter for further details.

Double Tiers

Where two tiers of the same size of a wedding cake are stacked to create the illusion of one tall tier.

Elbow

A veil that reaches down to the bride's elbows.

Embellishments

Adornments such as embroidery, lace, crystal beads, ribbons or pearls which are sewn onto a bridal gown.

Embossing

The raised three-dimensional imprint of a design, monogram, address or border sometimes used to embellish wedding stationery. See the *Stationery* chapter for further details.

Engraving

One of the most formal and expensive printing techniques used in wedding invitations. It is characterised by raised print on the front and an indentation on the back. See the *Stationery* chapter for further details.

Empire line

A high-waisted gown that flares out from just below the bust line.

Favours

Small inexpensive gifts given to all wedding guests to thank them for their attendance and to serve as a souvenir. (See *Bomboniere*.)

Finger Tip

One of the most popular lengths of veil which as the name suggests, extends to the fingertips.

Flat Printing

Also known as offset or lithography, the conventional flat printing technique is used for brochures and fliers. It is one of the few methods which allow you to use multiple ink colours in your wedding stationery. See the *Stationery* chapter for further details.

Flower Girls or Flower Children

Small children (usually girls) who pave the way down the aisle for the bride by holding a pomander or scattering flower petals from a small basket.

Flyaway

A many layered veil that barely reaches to the shoulder.

FMIL

Future Mother-in-Law. Acronym often used in newsgroups or email messages.

Fountain

A veil style where part is gathered on top of the bride's head, with the remainder set loose to fall around her face. A fountain veil will reach to either the shoulder or the elbow.

Ganache

A confection of cream and melted chocolate used as a filling between different layers in a single tier of cake.

Garland

Flowers and / or green leaves twirled into ropes or loops often used to adorn pews, staircases and doorways.

Groom's Cake

A smaller, second cake that may or may not be included in the wedding ceremony. It is often served at the rehearsal dinner.

Half Crown

An ornate headpiece for the bride which is between a crown and tiara in size and weight.

Halter neck

A backless style of dress which has a single strap which wraps around the neck, or a high-necked style with deep armholes.

Hand-Tied Bouquet

The *hand tied* or *natural stem* posy is a bouquet of long stemmed flowers tied together with a ribbon. Stems are bluntly cut for that fresh, just picked look.

Hen party

The bride's last night of freedom, traditionally organised by the chief bridesmaid.

Honour Attendants

The best man and the maid (or matron or man) of honour.

Latticework

A cake frosting technique that criss-crosses with an open pattern.

Lithography

Also known as offset or flat printing, this is the conventional printing technique used for brochures and fliers. It is one of the few methods which allow you to use multiple ink colours in your wedding stationery. See the *Stationery* chapter for further details.

Maid Of Honour

Known as the chief bridesmaid in some countries, she stands by the bride's side during the ceremony and holds the bride's bouquet during the vows.

Matron Of Honour

The proper title given where the chief bridesmaid is herself married.

Man Of Honour

Some brides prefer to have a male friend attending to the duties of the chief bridesmaid. If so, this is his title.

Mantilla

A Spanish word literally meaning 'little cloak', this is a lace or tulle shawl that the bride can wear around her head and shoulders.

Mantilla Veil

A long, Spanish-style circular or triangular piece of lace or tulle that is draped over the bride's head and held in place with a comb.

Marzipan

Made of sugar, egg whites and almonds, this substance can be used as a base for icing the wedding cake or to mould decorative forms such as flowers from.

Mermaid

A narrow, figure hugging style of dress that flares out just below the knee.

MOH

Acronym often used in newsgroups or email messages which stands for maid / man / matron of honour. See respective entries.

Nosegay

A small bunch of flowers and occasionally sprigs of herbs or berries tied or wired together. A popular choice for flower girls and bridesmaids.

Oasis

A hard, absorbent foam used by florists in bouquet holders or vases to keep flowers fresh.

Officiant

The cleric or secular official who carries out the marriage ceremony. In non religious weddings s/he might be a justice of the peace, magistrate or even the captain of a ship.

Off the shoulder

A neckline where the top of the gown's sleeves fall just below the shoulders.

Offset

Where cake tiers are placed at an angle or off centre to the other tiers.

Offset Printing

Also known as lithography or flat printing, this is the conventional printing technique used for brochures and fliers. It is one of the few methods which allow you to use multiple ink colours in your wedding stationery. See the Stationery chapter for further details.

Page Boys

Small children (usually boys) who follow the bride down the aisle often carrying some of her train.

Pillars

Also known as columns, they support and elevate the different tiers in a more traditional style of wedding cake design.

Pomander

A round ball completely covered in flower blooms sometimes carried by flower girls in the bridal procession.

Portrait

A wider version of the scoop neckline, falling at the tip of the shoulders.

Posy

A small, round, tightly packed flower bouquet that may include greenery or sweet smelling herbs.

Pouf

A piece of netting that is gathered up and attached to a headpiece or comb, to allow for extra height to the veil.

Presentation

An elegant bouquet of long stemmed flowers that the bride carries in her arms.

Ring Bearer

A small boy, or occasionally a girl, who walks down the aisle as part of the bridal procession carrying an ornamental cushion that has two rings tied to it. (Not the actual wedding rings).

Rolled Fondant

Sugar confection used to cover wedding cakes and create a soft, rounded edge to the completed design.

Scoop

A low, rounded, U shaped neckline.

Shantung

Similar to raw silk, shantung has a rough texture with irregular "nubbies" throughout the fabric.

Sheath

A narrow, figure hugging style of dress.

Shower

Also known as a cascade, this is a spray of long stemmed flowers often mixed with ivy which fall in a graceful waterfall shape.

Silk

An expensive, lustrous and fine but strong natural thread used for the most costly of wedding gowns. Satin, Organza, Chiffon, Shantung, and Velvet are some examples.

Spaghetti Straps

Thin, delicate straps which just support the bodice.

Square

A half square shaped neckline.

Stack Cake

Similar to the 'American' style, except each tier is the same width.

Stag party

The groom's last night of freedom, traditionally organised by his best man.

Strapless

A bodice without straps which finishes just above the bust.

Stroller Coat

A semiformal grey or black jacket resembling a tuxedo worn for daytime weddings.

Swag Effect

Icing, normally around the sides of the cake to create the effect of draped fabric.

Sweetheart

A neckline which dips to a heart shaped point in the centre.

Tails

An abbreviation for the tail coat worn for formal evening weddings.

Thermography

Currently the most popular choice for wedding invitations, thermography mimics the raised lettering effect of engraving but is much cheaper. See the *Stationery* chapter for further details.

Tiara

A thin jewelled semi-circular coronet with a higher front and sloping sides worn at the top of the bride's head.

Tiers

The numerous layers of a wedding cake, usually differing in size, which form part of the total design.

Topiary

The art of clipping or trimming foliage or flower arrangements so that they take on the shapes of animals, lettering, numbers, or various but precise geometric forms.

Tossing Bouquet

A copy of the bride's bouquet which she throws over her shoulder towards the female guests after the wedding ceremony. Legend has it that whoever catches it will be the next to wed.

Train

A long extension to a wedding gown that trails along the floor behind the bride.

Tulle

A fine mesh made from nylon, silk or rayon used for bridal veils and sometimes wedding gowns.

Tux or Tuxedo

A formal or semi-formal men's black evening jacket that may be either single-breasted (1-4 buttons) or double-breasted (2-6 buttons).

Vest

See *waistcoat*.

Vows

Promises of future loyalty, love, trust and support which lie at the very heart of the wedding ceremony. Vows may either be spoken as a statement or in response to the officiant's question.

Waistcoat

The vest worn over a gentleman's shirt and under his jacket for a formal evening wedding.

Waltz

See *Ballet*.

Wing Collar

The most formal type of collar, shirts with such collars are the standard choice for wearing with a tuxedo.

Wrap Around

A style of stack cake around which the icing is wrapped to create a soft "material drape" effect.

Wreath

A circle of flowers and /or leaves used as a centrepiece or above a doorway. It may also be referred to as a garland though there are slight differences. (See *Garlands*).

Acknowledgements

Many people have helped make the dream of this book a reality. In particular I would like to thank my amazing husband – thank you Rob for encouraging me to pursue my dream, and for your love, patience and creative input at every stage of this kit's production.

Thanks also to my parents Ed and Birgitta, for raising me to have the courage to dream and the confidence to put my ideas into action. The pride I saw in their eyes on my own wedding day will stay with me forever.

I am also gratefully indebted to my dear friend Michelle Crane, who even when she was planning her own wedding made time to edit this book. Without her help the result would not be anywhere near as professional.

Thank you also to designer Ailsa Easton, the most creative person I have ever known, for her loyal friendship and support throughout the writing of this book and her thoughtful suggestions for the 'What to Wear' chapter.

My heartfelt thanks also go to Jo Lawrence King for editing and proof reading this book, which I know was difficult to juggle with two small children.

And finally, thank you to florist extraordinaire Gwen Hands for her constant enthusiasm and original suggestions for the 'Flowers' chapter.

If you liked this book you might also enjoy...

One Stop Wedding Readings
by Jessica Howe

Celebrate your day your way – with words of love, wisdom and celebration!

Are you short on time? Grappling with how to express your thoughts on love, romance and marriage?

Then look no further. This unrivalled collection of over 100 of the world's finest readings and quotes contains blessings and good wishes for the bride and groom, moving poems and words to make you laugh. With One Stop Wedding Readings you'll discover how to:

- Eloquently express your deepest feelings about the unique love you share
- Harness the power of words for a wedding that oozes style, wit and emotion
- Captivate your friends with a personalised, memorable ceremony
- Save time you'd spend trawling the internet and hunting through bookshops
- Impress your guests with exquisite readings from every culture and era of history from Plato to Ghandi

Create an unforgettable wedding day full of wonder and joy with One Stop Wedding Readings.

Visit www.loveandcherish.net and order your copy today!

585392

Made in the USA